Transformation at Any Age

A Guide to Thriving Through Life's Transitions

Nova Kopp, Ph.D.

Published by ICXII Publishing
1348 Beach Blvd, Jacksonville Beach FL 32240 USA

ISBN: 979-8-9916585-3-9

Dedication

I dedicate this book to my mother, Odette Reynolds, who demonstrated unwavering strength and resilience. She came to this country without knowing the language, worked tirelessly, and built a successful business. She taught my siblings and me what it means to navigate life with courage and integrity.

And to my amazing husband, Mark Kopp, for being my hero and my rock, providing me with guidance and wisdom, and loving me as I am. Thank you for balancing me and standing by me through my life journey.

Special Acknowledgments

A heartfelt and enduring thank you to Dr. Bill McComb.

Your unwavering support, insightful guidance, and steadfast leadership were instrumental in shaping this book. Your ability to coach with both wisdom and compassion gave me clarity and confidence to bring this vision to life. You didn't just help refine the content you inspired the journey.

Thank you for believing in this work, and in me.

Authoring this book would not have been possible without the unwavering support, encouragement, and love of my family and friends.

To my family, thank you for your endless love and patience throughout this journey. Your belief in me gave me strength when I needed it most.

To my dear friends, Debra Adams, Angelique Langen, Lorraine Ryan, Richard Crain, and Susan Cagle, thank you for your valuable input, guidance, and encouragement that helped shape this vision into reality. I am forever grateful for your time, wisdom, and unwavering support.

To Scott Smith, Eliska Paratore, and every friend, mentor, and loved one who inspired me, lifted me, and reminded me of my purpose, thank you for being my anchor.

This book is as much yours as it is mine.

God Bless you,

Nova Kopp

Table of Contents

Introduction

Transformation at Any Age - Your Journey Begins

This book is based on my personal experiences but written for you. If you have ever felt stuck, broken, or lost, wondering why the same struggles keep resurfacing despite your best efforts, know that you are not alone. Life can derail us, and has a way of knocking us off course, either gently or forcefully. We all face setbacks, disappointments, and periods of uncertainty. When unhealed wounds, self-doubt, and unhealthy habits take root, it is easy to believe that real change is beyond our reach. I've discovered a powerful truth: Transformation is possible at *any* age, and in *any* season of life. As you experience the truths of this book, follow the process, and as you complete the exercises, you will discover a powerful truth. You are more than you realize; transformation is possible, and you will overcome life's most significant challenges, setbacks, and traumas.

Why This Book Exists

I did not grow up in a home; I grew up in a war zone. My childhood was shaped by the echoes of slammed doors, broken furniture, and the sting of both words and fists. My father, a Navy veteran, carried deep emotional wounds from his past. But instead of healing, he bled on everyone around him. His pain became our punishment. His trauma became our normal.

He was 6'2", towering in both presence and rage. When the switch flipped and it always did, we were powerless. He would hurl objects until the walls shook, and discipline us in ways that left more than bruises. He hit our heads together as if it were a lesson. He would explode over nothing. And some days, he would look at us like we were not even his children, just targets for the pain he could not name or control.

My mother, a 4'11" immigrant from Morocco, was the only line of defense. She stood between us and his fury more times than I can count. Her strength was quiet and sacrificial, but it could not protect us when he was in a rage. We had good days, but they were never safe days.

One of the most traumatic memories I carry is from seventh grade. When I got home from school, my father handed me a hammer and wanted me to kill a rabbit. I can still feel its weight in my hands. I can still hear the sound. I did not understand it then, and I do not fully understand it now. What I do know is that it did something to me. It broke something sacred. Today, I cannot even let a worm dry out on the sidewalk; I will stop and save it. That is how much this memory still lives in me.

But here is the truth: unresolved trauma does not fade; it festers. If we do not face it, we relive it. In our relationships, in our habits, and in the way we show up for ourselves and the people we love. I have seen what happens when people bury their pain. It does not go away; it goes underground and grows roots. I have seen people turn to drugs, alcohol, achievement, perfectionism, toxic relationships, and numbing behaviors because it is easier than confronting the truth.

That is why this book exists.

It is for the one who is tired of pretending everything is fine. It is for the one who wants to break the cycle but does not know how. It is for the one who has been surviving for so long that they have forgotten what it means to live.

Transformation At Any Age is more than just a self-help book. It is a blueprint for healing, reclaiming, and rebuilding a life that does not hide behind trauma but rises through it.

You are not your pain. You are not your past. You are not what was done to you. You are still becoming, and this book is your invitation to begin again.

The Leader's Realization That Changed Everything

Years later, I frequently led workshops on personal branding while working at AT&T. However, I noticed a more profound need: people were not simply looking for branding strategies; they were searching for clarity, confidence, and direction. Many possessed talent, drive, and ambition, yet something was holding them back. There was always a "but" attached to their name: "She's great at her job, but she lacks confidence." "He's got skills, but he struggles with self-discipline." "She's a strong leader, but her personal life is in chaos."

It became evident that individuals were attempting to establish success on unstable foundations. Before addressing personal branding, I needed to help them strengthen the core areas of their lives. I began taking them back to the fundamentals, the essential pillars that determine whether someone thrives or remains stuck.

Life as a Dashboard: The Five Areas of Transformation

Through my journey, I discovered that whenever I sought growth, improvement, or forward momentum, I had to assess five key areas of my life. These five areas became the framework for transformative growth, a personal dashboard that helps me navigate challenges, measure progress, and correct my course when necessary. Much like the dashboard of a car, which displays real-time data on speed, fuel levels, and engine performance, our dashboard provides insight into where we excel, where we struggle, and where we need to adjust in these five areas. This system includes a warning system categorized as follows:

- Green: Proceed. Everything is on track; you are thriving, hitting your goals, and making steady progress.

- Yellow: Caution. You need to regroup, re-evaluate, or adjust before things worsen. Yellow is a critical warning zone where awareness and action are essential.

- Red: Stop. Urgent attention is needed. If you do not make immediate changes, a breakdown is imminent. If you are in the red, it is time to stop. You must pause, analyze, and determine what's not working and begin implementing a new strategy.

These five areas of transformation are:

- **Spiritual Transformation:** Spiritual Transformation comes from utterly understanding and applying God's word as your North Star in life. The Bible provides wisdom, guidance, and the foundation for daily choices, reminding us to release what 'Holds You Back.' Engaging with scripture not only enhances your faith but also liberates you from hesitation, providing the tools necessary to navigate life's challenges with clarity and purpose. According to scripture, one can find strength, direction, and enduring transformation through God's word. When you are at the end of your life, you want to hear God say, "Well done, good and faithful servant!"

- **Physical Transformation**: Physical Transformation is taking care of your body. Prioritizing your health is essential for overall well-being. It is easy to fall into the trap of overworking, relying on caffeine, and sacrificing sleep. True transformation comes from balance, nourishing your body with proper nutrition, regular exercise, and adequate rest. A positive mindset toward self-care lays the foundation for lasting good health. Neglect your body, and it will eventually force you to slow down. Your body is the temple of your spirit.

- **Mental Transformation:** Mental Transformation is strengthening your mindset and attitude. True transformation begins in your mind. Your mindset shapes your reality. Mental growth means continuously learning, adapting, and strengthening your mindset to navigate change and adversity with resilience. It entails developing the discipline to control one's thoughts, modify one's perspective, and perceive challenges as opportunities for personal and professional growth. As a man thinketh he is, so put those guardrails up and protect your thoughts.

- **Emotional Transformation:** Emotional Transformation is about healing the heart and strengthening internal resilience. It is learning to respond to life with greater peace and maturity. It involves acknowledging past wounds and inviting God into the places that still hurt. It is allowing Him to replace fear, anger, shame, blame, and bitterness with His love, joy, and forgiveness. As emotional maturity develops, you become less governed by reactive feelings and more guided by inner calm and stability. Healthy emotional transformation enables deeper relationships and stronger boundaries and results in a heart that reflects the compassion of Christ.

- **Financial Transformation:** Financial Transformation creates stability for growth and begins with understanding the fundamentals of money management and making informed decisions that create long-term economic stability. The sooner you develop financial acumen and learn about savings, investments, and wealth-building strategies, the stronger your foundation will be for the future when you genuinely need security. Managing finances wisely and avoiding debt can help maintain financial stability. Transformation happens when you apply discipline, invest wisely, and position yourself for sustained growth.

Why This Matters

Transformation is not only about identifying areas for improvement; it is about having a system to measure and monitor progress, prepare for emergencies, and effectively use time, effort, and energy. Just like a driver who checks their dashboard before a long trip, you must regularly check in on your dashboard to ensure you are moving in the right direction safely and at the proper rate of speed.

What This Book Will Do for You

Consider this book as your North Star, a guiding light born from real-life experience and spiritual insight. Each chapter guides you step-by-step in strengthening the five pillars of your life:

- **Spiritual**: Find deeper faith and align your life with God's plan, purpose, and destiny.

- **Physical:** Achieve lasting health, energy, and stamina to sustain your life's mission.

- **Emotional:** Experience emotional peace, healing, and clarity by releasing stress and embracing purpose.

- **Mental:** Develop resilience, a growth mindset, and peace of mind through intentional thought renewal.

- **Financial:** Gain wisdom, stability, and freedom in your finances through biblical stewardship and intentional planning.

Transformation is a process requiring self-reflection, small intentional actions, and a willingness to build upon each lesson. This book offers practical tools for lasting change, including vision mapping, SMART goal planning, self-evaluation exercises, and biblical principles to guide you with wisdom and faith.

Why Faith Matters in Transformation

While many self-help books exist, true transformation, from my experience, lacks depth if one does not have faith. God's plan for your life is greater than anything you can imagine. Through scripture, prayer, and intentional growth, you will learn to trust His process and timing. ALS struck my family and shook my world. I had to rely on the foundation I had built on God's word. Without faith, I would have crumbled. The Bible says that when we are weak, He is strong. As we trust and believe, we can find strength in His presence during these moments of weakness and our most difficult challenges.

A Prayer of Healing and Guidance

Heavenly Father,

Thank You for this opportunity for transformation. Please give me the wisdom to recognize where I need to grow and the strength to act. Help me release fear, self-doubt, and anything holding me back. Let this be a season of renewal, healing, and breakthrough. I choose to trust You as I move forward in this process.

In Jesus' name, Amen.

How to Use This Book

Transformation At Any Age is not just a book to read; it is your personal journey toward excellence. More than just a book to read, it is an experience to engage with, reflect on, as you evolve into your true destiny. Each chapter builds upon the last, helping you create a solid foundation in every area of your life. You will reflect, set goals, and act. You will grow stronger spiritually, emotionally, mentally, physically, and financially. I encourage you to take your time, apply the principles, and trust the process.

Transformation is possible, but it requires commitment. It requires work. Are you ready to start your transformation journey? Let us build a solid foundation together.

Reflection Journal

How has adversity shaped your life?

_____

_____

_____

What areas need the most attention and growth?

_____

_____

_____

What do you hope to gain from this book?

_____

_____

_____

What specific goals do you want to achieve?

_____

_____

_____

My Journey: How I Discovered the Framework for This Transformational Process

My childhood involved instability, limited resources, and a focus on survival. I did not grow up with a roadmap for success. My father, haunted by the trauma of his past, carried wounds that became a burden on our family. After serving 22 years in the Navy, he struggled to find stable employment. His unresolved pain and financial hardship shaped my upbringing.

We lived in constant uncertainty. We minimized light usage to save money. We had running water, but we turned off the water heater to cut costs. There were times when the kitchen cabinets were bare, with only a single can of food left.

The car's gas tank was always empty. When we had gas, we were always mindful of how much we used. Each trip we went on was for essential purposes such as work, doctor's appointments, or necessary errands. My father even started raising animals for us to butcher, a practical yet painful reminder of how we scraped by. My mother worked tirelessly to hold things together, but the weight of our reality was overwhelming.

The day everything changed.

The Night My Mother Left

When I returned home one evening, I found my mother had left. There was no fight. No warning. There was no final goodbye. She just left. And she never returned. At first, I did not fully grasp what had happened. But as I stood in that house, I knew something was different. It was just me and my father now.

We had to walk miles to the store because there was no gas in the car. There was no browsing for goods, no picking out what we wanted. We purchased a cube steak and a potato based on our budget. That was our dinner.

I watched as my father carefully handed over crumpled bills at the register. His strong Navy hands trembled as he counted the change to make sure we had enough. That night, as we split our meal in the dimly lit house, I made a silent decision. I never wanted to live like this again. At the time, I did not know how to change my future. But deep inside my being, I just knew I had to.

The Night That Changed Everything

Two years later, when I was fourteen, my father took his own life. Grief settled over our family like a thick fog. My mother, now our sole provider, carried the weight of our survival on her back. Watching her, I learned what resilience looked like. My mother was resilient, not because she had a choice but because she had to.

Even as I absorbed her strength, I carried wounds of my own. I stumbled through my teenage years, lost, making mistakes, desperate for direction. Through all of it, one thing remained constant: my grandmother's faith. She had lost her son, yet she still prayed every night, trusting in God's plan. She taught me that even in darkness, there was always a way forward. At the time, I did not understand it. But the seed of faith she planted in me would one day change my life.

Drifting Through Life Without Direction

During my senior year of high school, everyone was talking about where they were going to college and what careers they wanted to pursue. I had no desire for college and had no idea what the future may hold for me. My family did not discuss college.

I ended up enrolling at Florida Community College at Jacksonville, not because I had a passion for education, but because I knew I could get a student loan, take the check, and run. I finished one semester, but my motivation had nothing to do with learning. If I went to campus at all, it was usually for a social event rather than class.

Then, I tried beauty school. That lasted about as long as it took me to realize I had no patience for the techniques. I was frustrated, could not grasp certain things, and quit. I had begun a cycle of attempts, failures, and discontinuation. Then came my first real job.

The Job That Opened My Eyes

At twenty-one years old, I took a job as a receptionist at Amerishare Investors, making seven dollars an hour. My car barely ran, and I parked at the back of the parking lot so no one would see it. I felt stuck, ashamed, and lost. But that job introduced me to people who were successful, financially secure, confident, and had purpose.

I started asking questions. How did they achieve success? What habits did they cultivate? What principles guided them? That was when I discovered the power of learning from those who had mastered transformation.

Seeking Knowledge: The Turning Point

I knew that if I wanted a better life, I had to change the way I thought. That realization led me to immerse myself in learning from the best. I studied Tony Robbins, Zig Ziglar, Tom Hopkins, and Suze Orman, soaking in their lessons on mindset, personal growth, sales, and fiscal responsibility. I realized that transformation was not just about working hard; it was about working smart, shifting my beliefs, and understanding how success worked.

Tony Robbins taught me about the power of emotional intelligence, goal setting, and overcoming self-imposed limitations. Zig Ziglar and Tom Hopkins helped me refine my ability to communicate, influence, and build confidence in my career. Suze Orman opened my eyes to financial literacy and the power of taking control of my money. I began applying these principles, and slowly, my life started changing.

The Birth of Transformation at Any Age

As I moved forward in my career, I started coaching and developing the best in people. I quickly realized something. Many people were struggling, not because they lacked skills or talent, but because they had unhealed wounds from their past. Their traumas, insecurities, and self-doubts seeped into the way they communicated, the way they managed challenges, and the way they showed up in their careers and personal lives. It was not about teaching them how to build a strong personal brand. It was, primarily, about addressing the underlying emotional and mental issues. I realized true transformation does not start with external change. It begins with addressing what is inside.

This revelation was the birth of "*Transformation at Any Age.*"

Prayer

Heavenly Father,

Thank You for guiding me to this moment. I know that my past does not define me, and with Your strength, I can step boldly into the future You have planned for me. Lord, help me to let go of anything that is holding me back: old wounds, fears, doubts, and the pain of yesterday. Please give me the wisdom to see the path ahead clearly and the courage to walk it with faith.

I surrender my plans, my struggles, and my desires to You. Align my heart with Your purpose. Please show me how to grow in body, mind, spirit, and stewardship. May my transformation help and uplift others.

I trust that You are making all things new in my life. I declare that I will not look back. I will press forward with hope, with strength, and with faith that You are leading me toward a life of purpose, fulfillment, and peace.

In Jesus' name, Amen.

Before You Begin This Journey...

I want to invite you to something more than just reading:

This book is not just information, it's transformation. And transformation begins with intention.

So, take a moment. Pause. Reflect. Write it down:

1. What are my top three priorities right now?

2. What is the most important thing I need to change in my life?

3. What am I willing to commit to over the next 90 days to move forward?

Keep your answers close. Revisit them often. Let them guide you as you rebuild, refocus, and rise.

Thank you for opening these pages and opening your heart. I believe in the work you're about to begin.

Chapter 1

Cultivating Self-Awareness: The Key to Lifelong Transformation

Jeremiah 29:11 (NIV): *"For I know the plans I have for you," declares the Lord, "plans to prosper you and not to harm you, plans to give you hope and a future."*

To understand the potential future ahead, it is essential to start with self-awareness and recognize who we are and how we can develop. This scripture reminds us of God's intentional and positive plans for our lives. Cultivating self-awareness is a crucial step in discerning and aligning ourselves with these divine plans. By understanding our strengths, weaknesses, values, and motivations, we can better navigate the path God has laid out for us and move towards the *"hope and a future"* He promises.

The Power of Self-Awareness

The power of self-awareness is transformative. Imagine living a life where you are entirely in tune with your emotions, strengths, and values. Picture yourself recognizing your triggers, navigating challenges with wisdom, and moving through the world with clarity and confidence. The power of self-awareness allows you to step into each situation with a deeper understanding of how your emotions influence your actions and how those actions impact others.

Have you ever known someone who sabotaged their own success in their career, relationships, or personal growth? Have you experienced repeated cycles, encountered similar challenges, and questioned why these issues persist? The common thread woven through these struggles is often a lack of self-awareness, the inability to recognize one's emotional patterns, strengths, and weaknesses.

A Personal Story: When Self-Awareness Changed Everything

I earned my undergraduate degree at 42 years old, not because I lacked ambition earlier in life, but because my journey unfolded differently. Looking back, I realize that self-awareness was the key that allowed me to achieve success with or without a degree. I understood my strengths, acknowledged my weaknesses, and, most importantly, I was coachable, teachable, open to innovative ideas, and could follow the direction and guidance of those who were more successful than me.

Some of the most successful people in the world do not have formal degrees, yet they thrive in business, leadership, and life. What sets them apart? High self-awareness. They recognize their abilities, seek feedback, and refine their actions accordingly. This ability allows them to navigate challenges, build meaningful relationships, and continuously improve.

Self-awareness is the foundation of emotional intelligence, leadership, and personal transformation.

Assessing Your Dashboard: The Traffic Light System

To effectively cultivate self-awareness, it is helpful to assess your internal state regularly. Think of it as monitoring your personal dashboard using the traffic light system. This concept uses the familiar traffic light colors to represent your current emotional and mental status:

Green Light: You feel good, focused, relaxed, and ready for any discussions or tasks. You are consistent with your core values and primary purpose.

Yellow Light: You are experiencing some discomfort or caution. This is a signal to proceed carefully and pay attention to your feelings and reactions before making decisions.

Red Light: You feel emotionally triggered. This is a sign to stop, step back, and reassess your state before proceeding.

Why Is This Important?

By consistently checking in with yourself using the traffic light system, you will cultivate greater mindfulness, achieve better emotional regulation, develop stronger decision-making skills, and improve your resilience.

What Are You Missing?

Lack of self-awareness can result in impulsive decisions that do not align with your values, struggles in relationships due to misunderstanding emotions, and repeating negative patterns without identifying root causes.

The development of self-awareness is essential. By developing it, we gain the clarity and courage to make choices that align with our true selves, creating a life of purpose and fulfillment.

What Does the Bible Say About Self-Awareness?

The Bible emphasizes wisdom, reflection, and aligning our actions with God's will. Self-awareness is a spiritual discipline that allows us to examine our hearts and grow in faith.

Lamentations 3:40 – *"Let us examine our ways and evaluate them and let us return to the Lord."*
Proverbs 4:7 – *"The beginning of wisdom is this: Get wisdom. Though it costs all you have, get understanding."*
2 Corinthians 13:5 – *"Examine yourselves to see whether you are in the faith; evaluate yourselves."*
Psalm 139:23-24 – *"Search me, God, and know my heart; evaluate me and know my anxious thoughts."*

Self-awareness is necessary for spiritual growth and for staying aligned with your faith.

What Is Self-Awareness?

Self-awareness is the ability to recognize and understand your own emotions, thoughts, and behaviors and how they align with your values and impact others. It is the foundation of emotional intelligence and lifelong transformation.

Two Types of Self-Awareness

Private Self-Awareness – Recognizing your internal emotions, reactions, and thought patterns. *Example:* Feeling anxious before a meeting and taking steps to manage it.

Public Self-Awareness – Awareness of how others perceive you. Your posture, demeanor, facial expressions, and body language may speak louder than your words. Example: Realizing that your tone of voice affects conversations and adjusting accordingly.

The Role of Humility and Self-Compassion

Humility allows us to accept feedback and grow.
Proverbs 11:2 – "*When pride comes, then comes disgrace, but with humility comes wisdom.*"

Self-compassion helps us overcome self-criticism and embrace imperfections.
Psalm 139:14 – "*I praise You because I am fearfully and wonderfully made.*"

Reflection Journal

- Past Feedback: What feedback have I resisted in the past? Why? What can I learn from this?

- Personal Strengths: What are my key strengths, and how can I leverage them more effectively?

- Areas for Growth: What areas do I need to develop to become a better version of myself?

- Emotional Triggers: What situations or people tend to trigger strong emotional reactions in me?

- Values Alignment: How well am I living in alignment with my core values? Where can I improve?

_____

_____

_____

- Action Plan: Based on my reflections, what specific steps can I take to cultivate greater self-awareness?

_____

_____

_____

_____

SMART Goal

A SMART action plan turns intentions into results. Here is an example:

- **Specific:** I will spend 5 minutes each evening reflecting on my emotional reactions and thoughts during the day. Clearly define the change you want to make.

- **Measurable:** I will document at least one key emotional reaction or thought pattern in a journal each evening.

- **Achievable:** Setting aside 5 minutes daily for reflection is a manageable time commitment.

- **Relevant:** The activity directly contributes to increasing my understanding of my internal state, which is a core aspect of self-awareness.

- **Time-Bound:** I will do this every evening next week. Assign a timeline to create urgency.

Now it is your turn. Set your own SMART goal below:

S – Specific:

_____

_____

M – Measurable:

_____

_____

A – Achievable:

_____

_____

R – Relevant:

_____

_____

T – Time-bound:

_____

_____

Prayer

Heavenly Father,

"Lord, search my heart and reveal areas where I need growth. Help me see myself as You see me with love, grace, and truth. Grant me wisdom to understand my strengths, courage to face my weaknesses, and discernment to navigate my emotions. Teach me to seek feedback humbly, to listen before reacting, and to grow in wisdom daily. May my self-awareness lead me closer to You and to the purpose You have for my life.

In Jesus' name, Amen."

Closing Thoughts

Cultivating self-awareness is a lifelong journey, not a destination. By embracing humility, seeking feedback, and engaging in regular self-reflection, we can grow in wisdom, deepen our relationship with God, and live more fulfilling lives.

DATE: _____

DATE: _____

Chapter 2

The Urgency of Change

Ecclesiastes 3:1(NIV): *"There is a time for everything and a season for every activity under the heavens."*

Change is an undeniable constant in life, flowing through our days like the turning of the seasons Solomon so wisely observed. While change happens all around us, true transformation, the kind that reshapes us from the inside out, is not automatic. It is optional, requiring a conscious decision to set out on an intentional path, recognizing that there is a season for growth, a season for pruning, and a season for a new beginning. Embracing the opportunities to implement change can lead us to a more purposeful, developed, and satisfying life, aligning us with the divine order of the world around us.

Embracing change is not always easy. It demands courage, self-awareness, and a willingness to face discomfort. Yet, when we embrace it, change becomes a catalyst for growth. This chapter will dive into why embracing change is necessary, exploring the hidden cost of staying the same, and how to start, even when it feels overwhelming.

The Hidden Cost of Staying the Same

Tony Robbins said it best: "Change happens when the pain of staying the same is greater than the pain of change." This profound statement encapsulates a fundamental truth about human motivation. Many of us resist change because it feels safer in our comfort zones, even when these are holding us back. We tell ourselves that it is "not the right time" or that "things will get better on their own". However, we secretly understand that maintaining the status quo often carries a higher cost than the benefits of directed change.

Ignoring the need for change does not make the problem disappear; it magnifies it. Whether it is a toxic relationship, poor health habits, or financial instability, avoiding action only allows the issue to grow. Over time, the hidden costs of inaction, regret, lost opportunities, and unrealized potential accumulate and become overwhelming. Studies show that people regret inaction more than actions they have taken, especially as they grow older. Missed opportunities often become the most significant sources of lifelong regret.

The price of inaction is not just a waste of time; it is lost dreams, lost relationships, and lost potential. Every day you wait is a day you could have moved closer to the life you desire.

The Pain of Staying the Same: Darla's Story

Darla was married to her husband for 18 years. He was a pastor, and they built a life together rooted in their faith and shared purpose. But one day, his revelation of his sexual orientation rocked her world. The revelation shattered everything Darla believed about her marriage and her life. She felt devastated, as if everything was unreal, a lie.

For years, Darla struggled with anger, grief, and a sense of betrayal. But over time, she realized that holding onto resentment was not hurting anyone but herself. She chose to forgive, not to excuse her husband's actions, but to free herself from the chains of bitterness. Eight years later, Darla is still on her journey of healing, but she has found peace. She has kept their family unit intact and chosen to walk forward with grace and understanding.

Darla's story reminds us that change is often painful, but it is also a doorway to growth. By letting go of what no longer serves us, we create space for something better.

Embracing Change: A Lesson in Adaptability

When I transitioned from a small, competitive local exchange carrier to Cingular Wireless, I knew I was stepping into a much larger organization. Still, I did not fully grasp what that meant until I experienced it firsthand. During a one-on-one with an executive early in my tenure, he gave me a piece of advice that stuck with me: "If you don't like change, this may not be the right place for you. This company is constantly changing." At the time, I nodded, not fully understanding the weight of his words. But every year, I saw it play out: annual reorganizations, new leadership, and shifting priorities. I felt like every time I got comfortable, everything would change again.

Initially, it was overwhelming, but over time, I shifted my mindset. Instead of resisting change, I started seeing change as an opportunity. A new supervisor provides an opportunity to gain experience from a different leader. A new team? It offered an opportunity to acquire new perspectives and insights. Rather than feeling destabilized, I learned to embrace change, recognizing that in a fast-paced organization, adaptability is a skill, not a burden, and necessary for success.

This experience taught me a powerful lesson about navigating change, not just in the workplace but in life. From a macro perspective, life itself is constantly evolving and changing. People leave us. Our bodies evolve. Our milestones shift. The seasons of our lives are continually in motion. If we do not learn how to navigate change with confidence, we will always feel destabilized, stuck in a rut, and missing our best life.

This realization became the foundation of my approach to transformation. Change is inevitable, but the way we respond to it is a choice. When we build a solid foundation physically, mentally, emotionally, spiritually, and financially, change becomes less of a disruption and more of an evolution. It is not about clinging to what was; it is about preparing for what is next. The key is not just accepting change; it is embracing it, trusting that each new phase brings opportunities for growth. By changing our perspective, we can make change happen for us. And when we do that, we step into a life of transformation at any age.

Removing the Chains: The Power of Forgiveness

Change often requires forgiveness for others and ourselves. It is essential to understand that forgiveness does not mean forgetting or condoning unruly behavior. It means choosing to release the anger and resentment that weigh us down. Without forgiveness, we stay trapped in the past, unable to move forward.

Forgiveness is the key that unlocks the chains holding us back and sets us free to pursue a brighter future.

Recognizing the Yellow Lights

Life often gives us signals. Yellow caution lights tell us when a change is necessary. These signals include:

- Feeling unfulfilled in your job or a relationship.

- Experiencing health issues due to neglect or poor habits.

- Struggling with financial problems, increased debt, instability, or stress.

- Feeling distant from God, your faith, or spiritual purpose.

When you notice these signs, please do not ignore them. Take a step back and ask yourself:

- What is causing this feeling of unease?

- What would happen if I stayed the same?

- What small steps can I take to move forward?

- What circumstances am I experiencing that are causing me to feel uncomfortable?

A Sense of Now: The Psychological Barrier to Change

Neuroscience research shows that our brain resists change due to its preference for comfort and predictability. However, experience shows that actual growth and fulfillment occur beyond this resistance. The longer you stay where you are, the harder it becomes to shift. Reframe your fear. Many times, the change you are avoiding is the breakthrough you need.

Creating Momentum for Change

The first step to change is often the most difficult. Starting the process of change can feel daunting, but small actions lead to significant transformations. Here is how to begin:

1. **Acknowledge the Need for Change:** Be honest with yourself about what is working and what is not working. Write down the areas of your life that feel stagnant or unaligned. Identify where you feel stuck.

2. **Define Your Vision:** What would success look like to you in this area? Be specific about what you want to achieve. Can you see yourself as 'successful' in this area of your life?

3. **Take Small, Consistent Actions:** Break your goals into manageable steps. Celebrate small wins along the way to build momentum.

4. **Focus on Solutions:** Instead of dwelling on the problem, channel your energy into finding solutions. Take time to brainstorm with yourself and with others. Remember, as Tony Robbins said, "By changing nothing, nothing changes."

5. **Find Accountability:** Share your goals with a trusted friend, mentor, or partner. Have them check in regularly on your progress and adjust as needed. Establish this as a new routine.

The Compounding Effect of Change

Think of change as compound interest: small actions done consistently create exponential results. The longer you wait, the more opportunities you lose. The most significant transformations do not happen overnight; they come from daily, intentional steps.

Journaling is a powerful tool to process thoughts, gain clarity, and track progress. Use the following prompts to reflect on your journey and create a personal roadmap for change. Write your responses on the lines provided.

Reflection Journal

What areas of your life are calling for change? Identify the yellow lights on your dashboard.

_____

_____

_____

What is holding you back? Is it fear, lack of knowledge, or resistance to discomfort?

_____

_____

_____

What is one small step you can take _today_ to start moving forward? Please write it down and commit to taking specific action.

_____

_____

_____

Describe an experience where you embraced change. What was the outcome? How did it shape you?

_____

_____

_____

What are three things you can do *this week* to move closer to your goal? Make a list and set a timeline.

_____

_____

_____

How does fear of change manifest in your life? Write about a time fear held you back and how you overcame it.

_____

_____

_____

Write a letter to your future self. Imagine yourself a year from now, having made the changes you seek. What would you tell yourself? What do you feel like?

_____

_____

SMART Action Plan

- **Specific:** I will identify one specific area in my life where I am resisting necessary change and write down three reasons why this change is important.

- **Measurable:** I will have one sentence clearly stating the specific area I need to change.

- **Achievable:** This task requires reflection and honest self-assessment, which is within my capability.

- **Relevant:** Understanding the urgency will immediately focus on my action in this area.

- **Time-Bound:** within the next 24 hours.

Now it is your turn. Set your own SMART goal below:

S – Specific:

_____

_____

M – Measurable:

_____

_____

A – Achievable:

_____

_____

R – Relevant:

_____

_____

T – Time-bound:

_____

_____

Prayer

Heavenly Father,

God, grant me the serenity to accept the things I cannot change, the courage to change the things I can, and the wisdom to know the difference. Identify areas of my life that need change and give me the strength to proceed despite fear. Please guide me to take small, consistent steps and remind me that with Your help, all things are possible.

In Jesus' name, Amen.

Closing Thoughts

Change is never easy, but it is always worth it. By recognizing the yellow lights in your life and taking intentional steps forward, you can break free from stagnation and create a life of purpose and fulfillment. Do not wait for the red light, but act now and watch how transformation unfolds. This is your moment. What will you do with it?

DATE: _____

DATE: _____

Chapter 3

The Five Pillars of Transformation: Building a Life that Lasts.

1 Corinthians 3:10-11(NIV) *"By the grace God has given me, I laid a foundation as a wise builder, and someone else is building on it. But each one should build with care. For no one can lay any foundation other than the one already laid, which is Jesus Christ."*

What Kind of Life Are You Building?

Each day, you are building something, brick by brick, choice by choice. Whether it is a career, your health, emotional well-being, or future, the fundamental question remains: What is your foundation? As Paul reminds us, neither the builder's skill nor the building's beauty matters if the foundation is unsound.

The Dome Structure: Five Pillars of Transformation

Picture a grand and majestic dome soaring toward the heavens. That dome stands strong only because it rests on a carefully engineered base with a solid foundation and supporting pillars.

In your personal transformation:

- Spiritual Foundation — the bedrock.
- Physical Pillar — your body and health.
- Emotional Pillar — your feelings and resilience.

- Mental Pillar — your mind and thought life.
- Financial Pillar — your stewardship and resources.

The dome representing your life, your legacy, and your impact is only as strong as the foundation and pillars beneath it.

The Spiritual Foundation is critical.

Without a strong, deep spiritual base, every other pillar is unstable.

Spiritual alignment strengthens your body, mind, emotions, and finances.

Each pillar supports the others, but the weight of the entire structure ultimately presses down onto the spiritual foundation.

Visual Description for Illustration

- Imagine a solid, wide foundation slab labeled "Spiritual Foundation."
- Rising from this base are four vertical columns, side-by-side but interconnected:
    - Physical (strength, health)
    - Mental (mind, wisdom)
    - Emotional (feelings, maturity)
    - Financial (stewardship, resources)
- Above the columns, resting securely is a dome labeled "Life and Legacy."

Each pillar is crucial, but the Spiritual Foundation must be strong for the structure to endure life's pressures.

Reflection Journal

• Which of your five pillars feels the strongest to you right now?

_____

_____

_____

• Which pillar do you feel God is calling you to strengthen next?

_____

_____

_____

• How might strengthening your Spiritual Foundation impact the other areas of your life?

_____

_____

_____

SMART Goal

Goal: Build balance across all Five Pillars.

- **Specific:** Identify one action to strengthen each pillar this month.

- **Measurable:** Journal weekly progress in each area.

- **Achievable:** Small, simple, meaningful steps.

- **Relevant:** Balanced pillars create a strong, enduring life legacy.

- **Time-Bound:** Review and adjust actions after 30 days.

Now it is your turn. Set your own SMART goal below:

S – Specific:

_____

_____

M – Measurable:

_____

_____

A – Achievable:

_____

_____

R – Relevant:

_____

_____

T – Time-bound:

_____

_____

Prayer

Heavenly Father:

Father, strengthen the foundation of my life, my spirit anchored in You. Help me tend to my body, mind, emotions, and finances with wisdom, purpose, and grace. Let my life stand strong through every storm, and let my legacy glorify You.

In Jesus' name, Amen

Closing Thoughts

You are building something every day, choice by choice. The five pillars: Spiritual, Emotional, Mental, Physical, and Financial, are for the structure of your life. They serve as your compass, your North Star. But without Christ as your foundation, even the strongest pillars would not sustain what you are building for yourself and for the generations to come. This process is not just about today. It is about the legacy you are preparing to hand off to your next generation. As Paul said, we must build with care. So ask yourself: What kind of life are you creating, and is it built to last?

DATE: _____

DATE: _____

Chapter 4

The Foundation of Spiritual Transformation: Laying Spiritual Groundwork for a Changed Life

Ezekiel 36:26 (NIV) *"I will give you a new heart and put a new spirit in you; I will remove from you your heart of stone and give you a heart of flesh."*

The Spiritual as the Core

Transformation, in its most authentic and enduring form, does not skim the surface of our existence. It does not begin with changing habits, reshaping our bodies, or even adjusting our thinking. True transformation starts deep within our spirit.

The Holy Spirit is the foundation upon which the entire structure of our life rests.

Like the sturdy base beneath a magnificent cathedral, our spiritual health supports everything: our physical strength, emotional stability, mental clarity, and financial stewardship.

Without a connected, vibrant spirit, breakthroughs are temporary, clarity fades, and behaviors eventually collapse under pressure.

Every lasting change in my life has not begun with external adjustments but with an internal, spiritual decision, a choice to surrender, listen, and align with God's wisdom.

When our spirit is anchored in Christ, life's storms may shake our surroundings, but they cannot uproot us.

A weak spiritual foundation leads to a transformation that is cosmetic at best.

It's like painting over rust, and the underlying damage eventually resurfaces.

But when our transformation flows from a deeply rooted spirit, everything else, physical health, mental peace, emotional strength, and financial wisdom, aligns and grows stronger

Our God centered spiritual foundation holds up the Five Pillars of Transformation:

- Spiritual (Foundation)
- Physical
- Emotional
- Mental
- Financial

The Spiritual Pillar lies at the base, the immovable, unshakable core sustaining everything built above it.

Reflection Journal

• When has a spiritual decision initiated a fundamental transformation in your life?

_____

_____

_____

• Where do you feel the most connected spiritually? Where do you sense God is calling you to deepen your spiritual life?

_____

_____

_____

• What daily practice could you commit to strengthening your spirit starting today?

_____

_____

_____

SMART Goal

- **Specific:** Spend 15 minutes each day in prayer, Bible reading, or stillness before God.

- **Measurable:** Journal three spiritual reflections weekly.

- **Achievable:** Set a daily alarm or dedicate a specific quiet time daily.

- **Relevant:** A strong spirit strengthens all other pillars of life.

- **Time-Bound:** Complete this practice for 30 consecutive days.

Now it is your turn. Set your own SMART goal below:

S – Specific:

_____

_____

M – Measurable:

_____

_____

A – Achievable:

_____

_____

R – Relevant:

_____

_____

T – Time-bound:

_____

_____

Prayer

Heavenly Father:

Anchor me deeply in You. Let my transformation begin at the very root of my being, my spirit. Strengthen me to withstand life's storms and grow me into the person You designed me to be. Shape my thoughts, feelings, body, and life from the foundation of Your love and truth.

In Jesus' Name, Amen.

Closing Thoughts

As we strengthen our spiritual foundation, we become more aware that our emotions are not obstacles; they are sacred messengers guiding us toward healing and growth. Let us now explore emotional awareness and how it echoes the soul.

DATE: _____

DATE: _____

Chapter 5

Physical Transformation: The Foundation of a Strong Life

1 Corinthians 6:19-20 (NIV): *"Do you not know that your bodies are temples of the Holy Spirit, who is in you, whom you have received from God? You are not your own; you were bought at a price. Therefore, honor God with your bodies."*

Every day, we make small choices that shape our future.

Some people wake up, drink water, stretch, and eat a nourishing breakfast. They feel alert, energized, and strong throughout the day.

Others skip breakfast, rely on caffeine, eat processed food, and struggle with fatigue. By mid-afternoon, they crash, mentally drained, physically exhausted, and struggle to push through.

The difference lies in our daily health habits.

Your body is either working for you or against you.

- When you care for it, you build resilience.

- When you neglect it, your energy declines and disease takes root.

Which path are you choosing? Ask yourself why you are on this path.

Why Physical Health Matters: A Biblical Perspective

Your energy, clarity, and longevity all depend on your physical well-being.

God calls us to honor our bodies, not to abuse them by making unhealthy choices.

Proverbs 23:20-21 warns against overindulgence: *"Do not join those who drink too much wine or gorge themselves on meat, for drunkards and gluttons become poor, and drowsiness clothes them in rags."*

Taking care of your health is not vanity; it is stewardship.

- People who prioritize their health experience consistent energy, mental sharpness, and strength.

- People who neglect their bodies suffer from chronic fatigue, brain fog, and declining mobility.

Your future self is watching the choices you make today.

Acknowledge the Challenges of Change

Change is never easy, and many struggle with obstacles like a lack of time, motivation, or resources. Overcoming these barriers requires intention, discipline, and small, consistent steps.

Small Changes, Big Impact

Lasting transformation does not happen overnight. Small, incremental changes lead to success, such as replacing soda with water, walking ten extra minutes a day, or preparing healthy meals. Compounded over time, these changes lead to lifelong vitality.

Accountability and Support

Change is easier with support. Find a workout friend, join a health-focused community, or work with a coach to stay on track. Encouragement and accountability can make all the difference in creating a healthy lifestyle.

Goal Setting for Success

Set realistic and achievable goals. Start with small, measurable targets, such as increasing daily steps, getting seven hours of sleep, and eating more fresh vegetables and healthy foods. Progress builds motivation. Believe in yourself, follow these steps, and become your own best health coach. Cheer yourself on with each success.

The Temple Analogy: Honoring Your Body

The Bible teaches that our bodies are temples of the Holy Spirit. What does it truly mean to treat your body as a temple?

- **Respect**: Avoid habits that harm your physical well-being, such as overeating, excessive alcohol, or neglecting exercise.

- **Nourishment**: Feed your body with lean protein, whole grains, fruits, and vegetables that provide energy and healing.

- **Restoration**: Prioritize rest, recovery, and stress management as essential components of honoring your health.

The "Bought at a Price" Aspect: Stewardship of Our Health

We are stewards of the bodies given to us. Recognizing that we were *"bought at a price"* means we have a responsibility to care for our health, not out of guilt, but as an act of gratitude and reverence.

Grace and Self-Compassion

Discipline is essential, but so is grace. Everyone experiences setbacks. The key is to learn, adjust, and move forward without guilt or self-condemnation. Progress is more valuable than perfection.

Incorporating Variety in Exercise

Physical activity should be enjoyable and sustainable. Explore different forms of movement:

- Walking or jogging in nature

- Strength training with bodyweight exercises or resistance bands

- Yoga or Pilates for flexibility and mindfulness

- Swimming or cycling for low-impact cardio.

- Dance, sports, or group fitness for fun and engagement.

- Consider joining the YMCA or a fitness club.

Rest and Recovery for Overall Wellness

Rest is a critical component of health. Incorporate these stress-management techniques:

- Deep breathing exercises to promote relaxation.

- Meditation and prayer to center your mind.

- Spend time in nature to reset and recharge.

- Engage in hobbies that bring joy and fulfillment.

Rest Is a Critical Component of Health

Rest is not a luxury. It is a necessity for physical, emotional, and spiritual well-being. In today's fast-paced world, intentional rest helps restore balance, renew strength, and calm the nervous system. Incorporate the following stress-management techniques into your daily routine to create space for peace, healing, and restoration:

• Deep breathing exercises to promote relaxation
Try **box breathing** (inhale for 4 seconds, hold for 4 seconds, exhale for 4 seconds, hold for 4 seconds) or **4-7-8 breathing** (inhale for 4, hold for 7, exhale for 8). These simple patterns slow your heart rate and quiet your mind.

• Use meditation or prayer to center your mind
Meditate on scriptures such as *Isaiah 26:3* — "You will keep in perfect peace those whose minds are steadfast, because they trust in you." Speak it aloud, reflect on each word, and breathe deeply as you allow the truth to settle in your heart.

• Spend time in nature to reset and recharge
A walk outside, even for 15 minutes, can lower stress levels, clear your thoughts, and help you reconnect with God's creation. Pay attention to His handiwork in the sky, the trees, or the sounds around you.

• Engage in hobbies that bring joy and fulfillment
Creative outlets like painting, gardening, journaling, or playing music can restore your energy and help you process emotions in a healthy way. Joy is healing and gives you strength—let yourself enjoy things that uplift your spirit.

Reflection Journal

Take a moment to reflect on how you currently manage rest and recovery. Use the space below to write honestly and prayerfully.

1. What does rest look like in your current routine?

_____

_____

_____

2. When do you feel most restored—physically, mentally, or spiritually?

_____

_____

_____

3. What is one unhealthy habit you can replace with a restful one?

_____

_____

_____

4. How do you feel after meals, and what patterns have you noticed in how different foods impact your energy levels, digestion, and overall well-being?

_____

_____

_____

Progress Over Perfection

Your health is a gift from God, your creator, and you have a responsibility to become and stay healthy and fit. There are no magic pills, but every step you take, no matter how small, moves you closer to your goal. Be intentional. Your future self is counting on you.

SMART Goal

- **Specific:** I will improve my physical well-being by eliminating processed snacks and eating whole, nutrient-dense meals.

- **Measurable:** I will prepare and eat clean meals at least 5 days a week and keep a short daily food and energy journal.

- **Achievable:** I will go to the grocery shop on Saturday and prep 3 meals in advance to reduce temptation and save time.

- **Relevant:** Eating well supports my energy, sleep, digestion, and my commitment to honoring my body as God's temple.

- **Time-Bound:** I will stick to the plan for 30 days and evaluate how I feel at the end of the month.

Now it is your turn. Set your own SMART goal below:

S – Specific:

_____

_____

M – Measurable:

_____

_____

A – Achievable:

_____

_____

R – Relevant:

_____

_____

T – Time-bound:

_____

_____

Prayer

Heavenly Father:

Thank You for the gift of my body, fearfully and wonderfully made. Forgive me for the times I have neglected or abused it out of stress, shame, or distraction. Please help me to see my health not as a chore, but as a form of stewardship. Please grant me the discipline to make better choices, the strength to overcome unhealthy habits, and the wisdom to listen to what my body needs. Remind me that transformation does not happen in giant leaps but in small, faithful steps. May I treat my body as a temple of Your Spirit, nourished, honored, and ready to serve.

In Jesus' name, Amen.

Closing thoughts

Your body is not just a vessel; it is a sacred gift. Every bite you take, every step you walk, and every habit you choose is either building you up or breaking you down. Physical transformation does not require perfection, just daily awareness and intentional care.

DATE: _____

DATE: _____

Chapter 6

Emotional Awareness:
Echoes of the Soul

Romans 8:26-27 (NIV): *"In the same way, the Spirit helps us in our weakness. We do not know what we ought to pray for, but the Spirit Himself intercedes for us through wordless groans. And He who searches our hearts knows the mind of the Spirit, because the Spirit intercedes for God's people in accordance with the will of God."*

Emotional transformation begins when we no longer suppress or ignore our emotions but allow the Holy Spirit to search, heal, and guide us through them. Emotions are sacred messages from the soul, alerting us to what needs healing, celebrating what brings us life, and pointing us toward our deepest longings and God-given callings.

While emotions are frequently seen as obstacles to success, Scripture teaches a different truth. Psalm 62:8 invites us, *"Trust in Him at all times, you people; pour out your hearts to Him, for God is our refuge."*

God welcomes our emotions. He doesn't reject or silence them. God uses them to speak to us, refine us, and draw us closer to His heart.

A song can awaken buried grief.

A scent can recall forgotten joy.

Silence can reveal inner peace we did not realize we needed.

Emotions are sacred clues to our soul's condition.

Mature emotional awareness involves acknowledging our emotions with empathy and critical judgment, ensuring that we neither allow them to dominate our actions nor disregard them completely.

It means asking questions like:

- Where did this emotion begin?
- What is it telling me about my heart?
- What healing or growth might God be inviting me into through this feeling?

As we become fluent in our emotional landscape, our spiritual foundation deepens. Healing emotions is part of healing the soul.

Reflection Journal

• What emotion do you find easiest to express? Which is hardest for you?

• Recall a time when God used an emotion to lead you to more profound healing. What happened?

• How can you invite God into your emotional life this week?

SMART Goal

- **Specific:** Set aside 10 minutes each evening to reflect on the day's strongest emotion.

- **Measurable:** Journal one emotional insight per day.

- **Achievable:** Use a simple journal or notes app.

- **Relevant:** Emotions are key indicators of spiritual and personal growth.

- **Time-Bound:** Complete this daily for 30 days.

Now it is your turn. Set your own SMART goal below:

S – Specific:

_____

_____

M – Measurable:

_____

_____

A – Achievable:

_____

_____

R – Relevant:

_____

_____

T – Time-bound:

_____

_____

Prayer

Heavenly Father:

Thank You for creating me with emotions. Teach me to listen to what my feelings reveal. Help me bring every emotion to You, the joyful, the painful, the confusing, trusting that You can heal and transform me through them.

In Jesus' Name, Amen.

Closing thoughts

As individuals increase their emotional awareness, they recognize that mental renewal is necessary for enduring change. Let us now focus on the daily renewal that restores our soul and reorients our thinking.

DATE: _____

DATE: _____

Chapter 7

Renewing the Mind, Restoring the Soul

Romans 12:2 (NIV): *"Do not conform to the pattern of this world but be transformed by the renewing of your mind."*

The invitation in Romans 12:2 is not a gentle suggestion; it is a powerful imperative. It speaks to the very core of our being, highlighting the critical link between our thoughts and behaviors. Renewing the mind is not a one-time event. It is a lifelong, daily decision to replace lies with God's truth and distortions with divine promises.

For many of us, the landscape of our mind is cluttered with debris, negative self-talk, limiting beliefs from childhood, past trauma, or words spoken over us that were never God's will.

Left alone, our minds repeat destructive stories:

- "I'm not enough."
- "It's too late for me."
- "No one sees me."

These become inner scripts that quietly dictate how we should be in the world, eroding our self-worth, stalling our growth, and holding us hostage from the life God intends for us.

But God's Word speaks a different reality:

- *"You are fearfully and wonderfully made"* (Psalm 139:14).

- *"You are chosen and dearly loved" (Colossians 3:12).*

- *"You are never alone" (Matthew 28:20).*

Renewing the mind means actively choosing which voice we listen to daily.

The late Dr. Charles Stanley said, "The mind is the control tower of your life." This truth can not be overstated. Your thoughts are not fleeting. They are the blueprint of your destiny. They fuel your actions, shape your emotions, and ultimately determine your path. Without guardrails, unchecked thought can reroute you away from God's best.

Scripture tells us this battle is spiritual. In 2 Corinthians 4:4, Paul writes that Satan blinds the minds of the unbelievers to the truth of the gospel. But it does not stop there. Even believers can be deceived (2 Corinthians 11:3) when we neglect the discipline of mind renewal through God's word.

Renewing the mind requires focus and spiritual intention. We must become the gatekeepers of our thoughts, rejecting what stems from fear, doubt, or worldly influence and embracing the truth God speaks over us.

"You are fearfully and wonderfully made." Psalm 139:14 This verse shatters the lie of inadequacy. You are not forgotten or flawed; you are a masterpiece created in God's image.

"You are chosen and dearly loved." Colossians 3:12 – This demolishes the belief that you are invisible or overlooked. God sees you, chose you, and loves you completely.

"You are never alone. God will never leave you or forsake you." God's Word refutes the lies of abandonment and rejection. God's presence is your permanent companion.

But renewing your mind is more than thinking right. It's about soul restoration. When our thoughts are wounded, our souls bleed too; shame, bitterness, regret, guilt, anger, and fear settle in. To be transformed, you must release these weights and replace them with grace, forgiveness, and hope.

Imagine pouring something precious into a cracked cup. No matter how valuable, if our vessel is cracked, it leaks. That is what happens when we skip renewing the mind with God's word. God can pour blessings, favor, and wisdom into our lives, but if our thoughts are broken, we cannot hold them—the blessing leaks.

When we do the work to renew our minds, God heals our souls. The cracks begin to mend. We become vessels of strength, capable of receiving, holding, and stewarding the blessings God pours into us with His love. As we renew our minds, real transformation takes root.

Reflection Journal

• What negative beliefs do you sometimes hear in your thoughts?

_____

_____

_____

• Which Bible truth can replace that lie starting today?

_____

_____

_____

• What would your life feel like if you fully believed God's truth about you?

_____

_____

_____

SMART Goal

- **Specific:** Identify one lie and replace it with one Scripture truth.

- **Measurable:** Speak it aloud or journal it each morning.

- **Achievable:** Use Bible verses you already know or search for new ones.

- **Relevant:** Renewed thinking leads to restored living.

- **Time-Bound:** Practice daily for 30 days.

Now it is your turn. Set your own SMART goal below:

S – Specific:

_____

_____

M – Measurable:

_____

_____

A – Achievable:

_____

_____

R – Relevant:

_____

_____

T – Time-bound:

_____

_____

Prayer

Dear Heavenly Father:

Renew my mind with Your truth. Let Your Word silence every lie. Heal my soul where fear, shame, or regret have left scars. Fill me with hope, peace, and vision as I walk in the freedom You died to give me.

In Jesus' Name, Amen.

Closing Thoughts

You may not be able to control every thought that enters your mind, but you can decide what stays. When you renew your mind with the Word of God, your life begins to reflect the heart of God. Your thoughts shape your life. Your life shapes your legacy. And your legacy matters. Be intentional. Be Bold. Be Transformed. Be Unstoppable. You start the process by renewing your mind with God's Word..

DATE: _____

DATE: _____

Chapter 8

Financial Transformation: Building a Strong Financial Future

Proverbs 22:7 (NIV) *The rich rule over the poor, and the borrower is the slave to the lender."*

Financial stewardship is not about numbers; it is about mindset, discipline, and faith. Wisely managing your finances is essential not only for achieving personal goals but also for preparing for life's unexpected challenges. This chapter explores the fundamentals of financial stewardship, highlights biblical principles, shares real-life anecdotes, and provides a clear roadmap for financial success at every stage of life, from your teens to retirement.

A Tale of Two Financial Paths

Let me share the story of two individuals, Lisa and Kevin, who perfectly illustrate the importance of financial stewardship.

Lisa earns over a quarter of a million dollars a year but struggles financially due to debt and overspending. She struggles financially, constantly juggling bills and feeling stressed about money. Kevin, earning $100,000 annually, owns his home, is debt-free, and enjoys financial freedom through diligent budgeting and wise planning. He regularly invests in his retirement and gives generously to his church and community. Their stories highlight that financial success is more about *how* you manage income than how much you earn. Lisa's problem is not a lack of income; it's a lack of stewardship and discipline.

Often, irresponsible spending and trying to buy or use things such as money and stuff to meet emotional needs and inner wounds fail, resulting in debt and more stress.

The Power of Compound Interest

Compound interest is one of the most powerful financial tools for building long-term wealth. It allows your money to grow not just from your contributions, but from the interest earned on those contributions, month after month, year after year.

Here are three real-life examples that demonstrate the importance of starting early and how regular saving can yield significant outcomes.

Example 1: Saving $100 per Month from Age 16 to 60 at 6% Interest.

If a 16-year-old saves $100 a month and earns an average annual return of 6%, by the time they reach age 60, their investment will have grown to approximately $258,426.

- Total out-of-pocket savings: $52,800

- Total value at age 60: $258,426

- Growth from compound interest: $205,626

That is the power of consistency and time. Even with modest monthly contributions, starting early multiplies your money in incredible ways.

Example 2: Saving from Age 16 to 30, Then Stopping

Now let's say the same teens save $100 a month but only until age 30, then stop contributing entirely. They leave the money invested at the same 6% rate and let it grow untouched.

- Value at age 30: $26,230

- Value at age 60 (no additional contributions): $157,975

Even though they only saved for 14 years and contributed $16,800, the power of compound growth turned that into nearly $160,000. Starting early, even for a brief time, can make a significant impact on your future financial well-being..

Example 3: Saving $100 a Month from Age 16 to 60 (7% Interest).

What if the average annual return was slightly higher, 7% instead of 6%?

- Total value at age 60: $352,535

- Total contributions: Still $52,800

- Growth of interest: Nearly $300,000

That 1% difference in interest, when combined with time, added almost $100,000 more to the total savings. Small shifts in rate and timing create massive changes in outcome.

Bottom Line: Start early. Stay Consistent. Let time and interest work for you.

Even lower amounts, when invested wisely, can build a strong financial future.

Let compound interest become your partner in financial freedom because your future is worth investing in.

Financial transformation begins with a shift in mindset:

- **Scarcity vs. Abundance:** A scarcity mindset ("I'll never have enough") leads to fear and anxiety about money. An abundance mindset ("God will provide, and I will be a faithful steward") fosters trust and generosity. Cultivating an abundance mindset involves focusing on gratitude for what you have, trusting in God's provision, and practicing generosity. It's about recognizing that true abundance comes from God, not from material possessions.

- **Instant Gratification vs. Delayed Gratification:** Our culture prioritizes instant gratification, which hinders long-term financial goals. Delaying gratification means making conscious choices to forgo immediate pleasures for future rewards. Focus on long-term financial security and practice self-control to strengthen this concept. It's about understanding that a small sacrifice each day can lead to significant gains tomorrow.

- **Emotional Spending:** Many people use spending to cope with stress, boredom, or other emotional issues and wounds. Identifying emotional triggers for overspending is crucial. Developing healthier coping mechanisms, such as exercise, journaling, or spending time with loved ones, can help break the cycle of emotional spending. Take time to pause. See the red light. Do some deep breathing exercises for a few moments, then ask yourself: "Am I buying this because I truly need it, or am I trying to fill an emotional void?"

- **Values-Based Spending:** Aligning spending with personal values brings purpose to financial decisions. What is profoundly important to you? Is it family, travel, or giving back to your community? Make sure your spending reflects your highest priorities. This might mean cutting back on non-essential expenses so you can allocate more money toward the things you value most.

Biblical Principles of Financial Stewardship

- **Be a Good Steward (1 Corinthians 4:2, NIV):** Manage resources faithfully. Use what God has given you wisely and responsibly, whether it's a little or a lot.

- **Avoid Debt (Proverbs 22:7, NIV):** Debt limits freedom; strive to be debt-free. While some debt may be unavoidable (e.g., a mortgage), prioritize paying it off as quickly as possible. Set up to autopay every two weeks and add $100 to the principal each time you make a payment.

- **Save and Plan (Proverbs 21:20, NIV):** Wise planning ensures future preparedness. Saving is not just about having money for emergencies; it is also about investing in your future and psychological peace, along with a financial backup plan.

- **Be Generous (Luke 6:38, NIV):** Generosity enriches both the giver and receiver. Giving should be a regular part of your financial plan. Tithing to your church is a biblical command, and in addition, we should support charitable causes. The Bible says to give, and it shall be given back to you. Give not only finances but also your time, effort, and support to others in the church and the community.

- **Work Diligently (Colossians 3:23, NIV):** A committed and disciplined work ethic leads to financial stability. A strong work ethic is essential for building a solid financial foundation. Use wisdom to balance your work life and your family time.

- **Trust God (Philippians 4:19, NIV):** Trust God's provision while managing finances wisely. Financial stewardship is about balancing wise planning with faith in God's provision. Remember that Deuteronomy 8:18 states, "*that God gives us the power to create wealth.*"

- **Avoid Love of Money (1 Timothy 6:10, NIV):** Prioritize faith and purpose over wealth. Money is a tool, not a goal. Do not let the pursuit of wealth become an idol.

Practical Financial Fundamentals

- **Budgeting:** Create and revise a detailed monthly budget, including all income and expenses. Track your spending using apps like Mint or YNAB (You Need a Budget). The 50/30/20 rule (50% needs, 30% wants, 20% savings/debt repayment) can be a helpful guideline. Consider the teachings of Dave Ramsey.

- **Debt Reduction:** Use the debt snowball (small debts first) or avalanche (highest interest first) method. Negotiate lower interest rates with creditors. Address the root causes of your debt – are you overspending in certain areas? Consider these additional strategies:

  - **Debt Consolidation:** Combine multiple debts into one with a lower interest rate.

  - **Balance Transfer:** Transfer high-interest credit card balances to a card with a 0% introductory APR.

- o **Debt Management Plan:** Work with a credit counseling agency to create a plan for repaying your debts.

- o **Have a Delay Spending Plan:** Create a 3 to 7-day waiting period before spending on any nonessential items. Monitor your online purchases and money spent on meals, delivered, or while eating out at restaurants. Set a budget.

- **Savings:** Aim to save at least 20% of your income. Build an emergency fund (3-6 months of living expenses) in a readily accessible account. Set up automatic transfers to your savings account.

- **Investing:** Diversify across different asset classes:

  - o **Stocks:** Represent ownership in a company. Potential for higher returns but also higher risk.

  - o **Bonds:** These are loans to a company or government. In general, bonds are less risky than stocks, but they offer lower potential returns.

  - o **Real Estate:** Investing in property can provide rental income and potential appreciation.

- **Index Funds/ETFs:** Baskets of stocks or bonds that track a specific market index (e.g., the S&P 500) offer diversification and low costs.

- **Mutual Funds:** Professionally managed funds that pool money from multiple investors. Consider your risk tolerance and investment goals when choosing investments. For beginners, starting with low-cost index funds or ETFs can be a beneficial approach. Understand the power of compound interest – your money earns interest, and then the accumulated interest earns interest, leading to exponential growth over time.

- **Children's Funds:** Open 529 plans or custodial accounts (UGMA/UTMA) for college savings. Start teaching your children about money management early.

Financial Milestones Across Life Stages

- **Teens (13-19):**

  - **Financial Literacy:** Learn the basics of budgeting, saving, and responsible credit use. Open a bank account and get comfortable managing your own money.

  - **Earning and Saving:** Start earning money through part-time jobs or chores.

Develop a saving habit by setting aside a portion of your earnings.

- **Understanding Credit:** Learn about credit scores and how they work. Avoid taking on unnecessary debt.

- **Young Adults (20-29):**

  - **Building Credit:** Establish good credit by using a credit card responsibly and paying your bills on time. Consider paying off each month's credit card charges altogether. This practice will eliminate high credit card interest rates and will help you monitor your spending.

  - **Debt management:** Avoid high-interest debt (e.g., payday loans). Start paying off any student loans or other debt.

  - **Investing Early:** Start investing, even in lesser amounts, to take advantage of compound interest. Consider opening a Roth IRA.

  - **Emergency Fund:** Build a small emergency fund to cover unexpected expenses.

- **Mid-Career (30-49):**

  - **Retirement planning:** Maximize contributions to retirement accounts

(401(k), IRA). Collaborate with a financial advisor to create a retirement plan.

- o **Mortgage Management:** If you own a home, develop a plan to pay off your mortgage. Paying an extra $100 on your mortgage each month towards the principal will save you thousands.

- o **Education Planning:** If you have children, start saving for their college education using 529 plans or other investment vehicles.

- o **Insurance:** Ensure you have adequate insurance coverage (health, life, disability).

- **Pre-Retirement (50-64):**

Retirement review: Evaluate your retirement plan and make any necessary changes.

- o **Debt reduction:** Aim to pay off all debt, including your mortgage, cars, and credit cards, before retirement.

- o **Long-Term Care:** Consider purchasing long-term care insurance to protect against future healthcare costs.

- o **Estate Planning:** Create or update your will and other estate planning documents.

- o **Other Documents:** Ensure that all medical paperwork is complete, including end-of-life documents, do-not-resuscitate orders, and powers of attorney. Ensure proper execution and secure storage.

- **Retirement (65+):**

  - **Investment management:** Manage your retirement investments and create a withdrawal strategy.

  - **Healthcare Costs:** Plan for healthcare expenses, including Medicare and supplemental insurance.

  - **Legacy Planning:** Consider how you want to leave a legacy for your family and community.

  - **Enjoyment:** Make sure to enjoy your retirement and the financial freedom you have worked so hard to achieve.

  - **Military:** If you have prior military service, please check with the Veterans Administration for any benefits and/or healthcare coverage.

  - **Advisors:** Seek assistance and get advice from qualified financial advisors.

Reflection Journal

Budgeting Insights: What areas did you overspend in last month? How can you adjust your budget? Who can be an accountability partner to help you be more responsible in your spending and debt reduction?

_____

_____

_____

Debt Reduction Progress: What steps have you taken to reduce your debt? What is your next target? Make a detailed list of all debts, interest rates, and monthly payment amounts, and create a reasonable plan to begin eliminating all debts.

_____

_____

_____

Investment Research: What investments are you considering? Why?

_____

_____

_____

Retirement Planning: Have you calculated your retirement needs? What steps are you taking to reach your goal?

_____

_____

_____

SMART Goal

- **Specific:** I will save $10,000 for a car down payment.

- **Measurable:** I will track my savings progress monthly.

- **Achievable:** I will set aside approximately $1,667 per month by adjusting my budget and cutting nonessential expenses.

- **Relevant:** This goal supports my goal of getting a new car

- **Time-bound:** I will reach my $10,000 savings goal. Set deadlines for each goal.

Now it is your turn. Set your own SMART goal below:

S – Specific:

_____

_____

M – Measurable:

_____

_____

A – Achievable:

_____

_____

R – Relevant:

_____

_____

T – Time-bound:

_____

_____

Prayer

Dear Heavenly Father:

Please guide me in managing my finances with wisdom and faith. Help me to be a faithful steward of all that You have entrusted to me. Grant me discipline to budget, strength to avoid debt, and wisdom to invest for the future. Fill my heart with generosity and trust in Your provision. May my financial journey reflect Your glory, and may I bless others through my financial decisions.

In Jesus' name, Amen.

Closing Thoughts

During a period of unexpected job loss, the financial habits my family had built, like budgeting wisely and saving diligently, became a lifeline. Because we had lived within our means and prioritized a 6-month emergency fund, we were able to weather the storm without falling into debt. That experience did not just reinforce the importance of financial stability; it reminded us of the peace that comes from trusting God and stewarding well what God has entrusted to us.

Financial transformation is not just about income or numbers. It is about mindset, discipline, and faith. When we manage our resources with intentionality and wisdom, we honor God and create margin for generosity, peace, and long-term stability. Here are a few practical resources I have found helpful:

- **Budgeting Apps:** YNAB (You Need a Budget), Mint, Every Dollar

- **Investment Platforms:** Vanguard, Fidelity, Schwab, Robinhood

- **Financial Websites:** Investopedia, NerdWallet, The Balance

- **Retirement Calculators:** Choose a reputable calculator from a trusted source like Fidelity, Schwab, or Vanguard.

DATE: _____

DATE: _____

Chapter 9

Building Your Vision:

Habakkuk 2:2 (KJV) *"And then the Lord answered me, and said, Write down the vision and make it plain upon the tables, that he may run who reads it."*

When God instructed Habakkuk to write the vision, He wasn't just giving him a task. He was providing a strategy for making the unseen visible.

Vision gives our hearts direction. It fuels our faith and keeps us moving forward even when the road gets tough.

Creating a vision board or writing out your dreams plainly is a practical way to honor this principle.

It brings clarity, focus, and spiritual agreement to the promises God has planted within us.

Why Vision Boards Work

- Focus: Keeps your mind centered on God's promises, not your fears.

- Daily reminder: What is unseen will come to life in God's timing.

- Mental Priming: Neuroscience shows that visual reminders strengthen motivation and confidence.

- Emotional Engagement: Seeing the dream awakens hope and energizes perseverance.

Ways to Create Your Vision Board

Everyone's approach is different, and that is beautiful. Here are a few ways:

1. **Visual Collage:** Cut out pictures from magazines or print images that represent your goals. Glue them to a board or canvas. Add scriptures next to images that confirm your dreams.

2. **Written Vision Statement:** Write your vision in powerful, first-person, present-tense sentences. Surround your words with scriptures. This is the method I used, a written vision anchored in God's promises.

3. **Hybrid Board:** Combine visuals and written prayers. Group them into categories like Spiritual, Physical, Emotional, Mental, and Financial goals.

4. **Digital Vision Board:** Use online tools like Canva or Pinterest to build a board you can save on your phone or computer for daily inspiration.

Reflection Journal

• What areas of your life do you want to reflect God's vision more clearly?

_____

_____

_____

• What scriptures support the dreams and goals God has placed in your heart?

_____

_____

• Which style of vision board (visual, written, hybrid, or digital) feels right for you?

SMART Goal

- **Specific:** Choose a method and begin gathering materials today.

- **Measurable:** Complete your board within 7 days.

- **Achievable:** Dedicate 30–60 minutes to start simple.

- **Relevant:** Keeps God's promises visible and active in your daily life.

- **Time-Bound:** Refresh or update your board every 3–6 months.

Now it is your turn. Set your own SMART goal below:

S – Specific:

_____

_____

M – Measurable:

_____

_____

A – Achievable:

_____

_____

R – Relevant:

_____

_____

T – Time-bound:

_____

_____

Prayer

Dear Heavenly Father:

Lord, thank You for the dreams and visions You have placed within me. Please help me to write the vision, make it plain, and run with it in faith. Let my heart stay full of hope, my mind clear with purpose, and my steps guided by Your Spirit.

In Jesus' name, Amen.

Closing thoughts

By grounding ourselves and clarifying our vision, we prepare to build strong lives supported by five pillars: spiritually grounded, physical health, emotional resilience, mental clarity, financial wisdom, and personal integrity.

DATE: _____

DATE: _____

Chapter 10

Setting Goals: A Roadmap to Success

Proverbs 16:3 (NIV) Commit to the Lord whatever you do, and He will establish your plans."

The Power of Goal Setting

Change alone is not enough; you need a clear path forward to ensure that your transformation is intentional and sustainable. Goal setting provides direction, helping you turn aspirations into actionable steps that lead to measurable success. Without structure, goals can feel overwhelming, vague, or unattainable, leaving you stuck in a cycle of wishing rather than achieving.

Having a written plan keeps you focused, motivated, and accountable. It allows you to measure your progress, adjust when necessary, and ensure that your daily actions align with the life you want to create.

The Power of Writing Down Your Goals

Goals **are critically important**. Writing them down is more than just an exercise. It is a **declaration of intent**. The Bible affirms this principle in **Habakkuk 2:2**, which reminds us to: *"Write the vision; make it plain on tablets."*

Writing down your **vision** helps bring **clarity, focus, and accountability**.

For the past 30 years, I have been intentional about setting goals in five key areas: spiritual, physical, mental, emotional, and financial. I do not just think about my goals; I write them down and commit to them.

- **Physical**: Lose five pounds, eat healthy six days a week with one cheat day, exercise 3 to 5 times a week.

- **Emotional:** Grow in emotional resilience by identifying triggers, processing emotions with grace, and responding with spiritual maturity.

- **Mental**: Strengthen focus and clarity by renewing my mind through learning, self-discipline, and intentional thought patterns.

- **Spiritual**: Attend church regularly, read the Bible, and volunteer in the community.

- **Financial**: Save a specific amount, invest wisely, and eliminate debt.

I break my goals into **actionable steps**. This is what I have learned:

When you write your goals down, something shifts in your brain. It is like setting a GPS destination. Your subconscious mind begins to align your actions with your vision.

A Real-Life Example: The Power of Written Goals

Throughout my career, I have coached many people, and one experience stands out. While working at AT&T,

I coached a gentleman we will call John. He wanted to move up in the company, and we often discussed his brand, strengths, and areas where he needed to improve.

One day, I challenged him: *"Write down your goals clearly, put them in your wallet, and carry them with you every day."*

At first, he did not do it. Weeks went by. I reminded him, and he kept putting it off.

Then, one day, John walked over to my desk and asked: *"Can we go to lunch? I have something to share with you."*

As we sat down, he grinned and said: *"I got promoted."*

Then, he pulled out his wallet, unfolded a small piece of paper, and showed me his written goal.

There it was, clear, intentional, and now achieved.

That moment reinforced what I had always believed: Writing down your goals makes them real, tangible, powerful, and attainable.

When you see your goals every day, they become part of your subconscious. You naturally start making decisions that bring you closer to achieving them. John's story proves that when you commit to a vision and take consistent action, success follows.

When Goal Setting Changed My Life: A Personal Story

Years ago, I found myself stuck, neither failing nor progressing. I had dreams: earning my degree, becoming financially stable, and improving my health. Yet, without a clear plan, I kept putting things off, waiting for the "right moment."

Then, a mentor asked me a question, challenging me, and this changed everything:

"What is stopping you? If you don't set a deadline, you'll wake up in five years and be in the same place."

That moment hit me hard. I realized that change was not just going to happen; I had to make it happen. I sat down, wrote out my goals, set realistic timelines, and broke them down into small, actionable steps.

At first, the process felt overwhelming. But step by step, I started seeing the results:

- I earned my undergraduate degree at 42.

- I paid off my debt and achieved financial independence.

- I became committed to my physical and spiritual well-being.

None of these accomplishments happened accidentally; they were the result of intentional goal setting. That is what I want to share with you today: a roadmap to success that will help you set, track, and achieve your goals with confidence.

Reflection Journal

1. Identifying Your Growth Areas

What is one specific area in your life where you want to see significant growth or change?

_____

_____

_____

2. Defining Success

What does success look like in this area? What specific outcomes do you want to achieve?

_____

_____

_____

3. Overcoming Obstacles

_____

_____

What potential obstacles might hinder your progress, and how can you proactively address them?

_____

_____

_____

4. Finding Accountability

Who can you share your goals with for support and accountability? How will you track your progress and celebrate milestones?

_____

_____

_____

SMART Goal:

- **Specific:** I want to work on my Spiritual Pillar by waking up at 6:30 a.m. on weekdays, spending 30 minutes with the Lord.

- **Measurable:** 30 minutes a day, 5 days a week

- **Achievable:** 6:30 a.m. is a realistic time that fits my schedule.

- **Relevant:** The habit will strengthen my spiritual focus and daily discipline.

- **Time-Bound:** I will do this for 4 weeks starting Monday.

Now it is your turn. Set your own SMART goal below:

S – Specific:

_____

_____

M – Measurable:

_____

_____

A – Achievable:

_____

_____

R – Relevant:

_____

_____

T – Time-bound:

_____

_____

Prayer

Dear Heavenly Father:

"Lord, I thank You for the vision You have placed in my heart. Help me to set goals that align with Your purpose for my life. Please give me the wisdom to plan wisely, the discipline to act, and the perseverance to follow through. Strengthen my faith so that I may trust Your timing. Remind me that every step I take brings me closer to my God-given destiny, You have prepared for me. Guide me to seek clarity, stay focused, and honor You in my work.

In Jesus' name, Amen."

Closing thoughts

Setting goals is not just about achieving short-term success; it is about developing habits that lead to lifelong transformation. The goals you set today should:

- Challenge you to grow.

- Stretch you beyond your comfort zone.

- Inspire you to become the person you were created to be.

*"**Your decisions shape your destiny.**"* Tony Robbins

DATE: _____

DATE: _____

Chapter 11

My Journey with Resilience

Corinthians 4:8-9 (NIV): We are hard pressed on every side, but not crushed; perplexed, but not in despair; persecuted, but not abandoned, struck down, but not destroyed."

I learned the true meaning of resilience when my life took an unexpected and overwhelming turn. In a short span of time, my husband received a diagnosis of ALS, and my mother suffered a stroke. Overnight, I went from managing my personal and professional life to becoming a full-time caregiver. My priorities underwent significant changes, necessitating the making of unforeseen life-altering decisions.

I retired early and moved to Jacksonville to create a safe and accessible space for my husband and mother. My days consisted of appointments, therapy, and constant change. We modified our home for medical equipment, arranged transportation to appointments, and did my best to balance my emotions while caring for them both.

At first, it was overwhelming. The weight of it all felt crushing. I had moments where I questioned my ability to manage it all and if I was strong enough, patient enough, and resilient enough. But in those moments of doubt, I realized something:

True resilience lies in adapting to daily life challenges and trusting God. It is about showing up, even when you do not feel ready. It is about enduring hardship, growing through it, and tapping into my God-given strength to do whatever is necessary.

There were days I felt drained, unseen, and exhausted beyond words. One particularly difficult night, after hours of caregiving, I found myself sitting in the dark, consumed by fear and uncertainty. I whispered, "I don't know if I can do this." Deep within my heart, I heard *2 Timothy 1:7: "God has not given us a spirit of fear, but of power, love, and a sound mind."* Love. Power. A sound mind. Not fear. Speaking those words aloud shifted my mindset. I was not alone. God had already given me the strength I needed.

Breaking Through Self-Doubt and Mental Barriers

One of the biggest obstacles to resilience is self-doubt. Self-doubt tells us we are not strong enough, not capable enough, not ready. It keeps us stuck in fear instead of moving us forward in faith.

I remember one challenging day when my husband was in a lot of pain, and I felt utterly overwhelmed. The negative thought screamed in my head: "I cannot do this. I am not strong enough." But once again, in that moment, I remembered 2 Timothy 1:7: *"God has not given us a spirit of fear, but of power, love, and a sound mind."* I repeated that verse over and over until the fear began to subside, and I found the strength to keep going.

Resilience Across Life's Ages

Teens (Ages 13-18): Learning to Face Challenges

The teenage years are a training ground for resilience and adapting to change. It is crucial to understand that a failing test grade or a failure in sports does not define your worth. It is essential to acknowledge that setbacks are opportunities for growth.

"I can do all things through Christ who strengthens me" (Philippians 4:13).

This verse of Scripture is a powerful affirmation during these times of self-discovery and pressure. Developing confidence by tackling small obstacles like speaking up in class or mastering a new skill builds a foundation for future challenges. Learning healthy emotional regulation through journaling, prayer, or talking to a trusted adult equips teens to navigate the emotional rollercoaster of adolescence.

Young Adults (Ages 19-35): Navigating Transitions

These years bring uncertainty and change. Facing career setbacks, managing financial stress, and striving for independence all test our resilience. Leaning on Proverbs 3:5-6, *"Trust in the Lord with all your heart and lean not on your own understanding, in all your ways acknowledge Him and He shall direct your path,"* can provide comfort. Seeking guidance from mentors, setting achievable goals, and developing a mindset of perseverance help navigate these challenges.

Middle adulthood (Ages 36-55): Balancing Responsibilities

Managing work-life balance, relationships, and personal well-being requires adaptability. It is easy to become overwhelmed, but resilience comes from setting boundaries, prioritizing what truly matters, and seeking strength in faith. Psalm 55:22 reminds us to *"Cast your burden on the Lord, and He will sustain you."* Finding purpose beyond career success through mentoring, volunteering, or faith-based service adds fulfillment beyond professional accomplishments.

Older Adults (Ages 56+): Embracing Change & Legacy

Aging brings transitions but also wisdom.

Isaiah 46:4 reassures that *"Even to your old age and gray hairs I am He, I am He who will sustain you."*

Finding peace in changing roles, adapting to physical limitations, and leaving a legacy through mentorship or storytelling can be deeply fulfilling.

Building a Strong Support System

I remember when my mother had her first stroke; I felt utterly alone. But then, a friend from church started bringing meals over. Even though it was such a small gesture, it had a profound impact. Knowing that someone cared and was there for me gave me the strength to keep going. It was not just the practical help; it was the emotional support, the feeling that I was not carrying this burden alone, that truly lifted me. Ecclesiastes 4:9-10 reminds us: *"Two are better than one... If either of them falls, one can help the other up."*

Reflection Journal

1. Describe the specific challenges you faced:

_____

_____

_____

2. What were your initial emotional responses?

_____

_____

_____

3. What scripture or aspect of your faith did you apply to navigate the situation?

_____

_____

_____

4. How can this experience strengthen your spiritual, emotional, or mental growth?

_____

_____

_____

Identify a moment when you experienced self-doubt. What scripture or word of encouragement could help you move through it with faith and confidence?

_____

Think of someone who supported you during a tough time. How did their kindness impact your journey, and in what way did it help you move forward?

SMART Goal:

- **Specific:** I want to work on my Spiritual Pillar by waking up at 6:30 a.m. on weekdays, spending 30 minutes with the Lord.

- **Measurable:** 30 minutes a day, 5 days a week

- **Achievable:** 6:30 a.m. is a realistic time that fits my schedule.

- **Relevant:** The habit will strengthen my spiritual focus and daily discipline.

- **Time-Bound:** I will do this for 4 weeks starting Monday.

Now it is your turn. Set your own SMART goal below:

S – Specific:

_____

_____

M – Measurable:

_____

_____

A – Achievable:

_____

_____

R – Relevant:

_____

_____

T – Time-bound:

_____

_____

Prayer

Heavenly Father:

I come before You, seeking strength and guidance as I navigate the challenges in my life. Thank You for the strength You have already given me to face these challenges. Help me cultivate patience, endurance, and faith. Grant me wisdom to discern what I can control and the courage to let go of what I cannot. Surround me with Your peace and equip me with resilience to face each day. I trust that You are using these challenges to shape me into who You have called me to be.

In Jesus' name, Amen.

Closing Thoughts

Resilience is not a destination; it is a journey of growing stronger from each situation and gaining strength. It involves addressing challenges with confidence and adaptability. By leaning on God's promises, building a dedicated support system, and practicing the principles outlined here, you can cultivate resilience, and you will not just survive but thrive, even when life gets tough. Resilience is not about never falling. It is having the courage to face challenges, adapt, and rise stronger, grounded in faith and trust in God.

DATE: _____

DATE: _____

Chapter 12

Overcoming Obstacles, Building Resilience

Isaiah 40:31 (NIV): *"But those who hope in the Lord will renew their strength. They will soar on wings like eagles; they will run and not grow weary; they will walk and not be faint."*

Resilience is not about avoiding adversity; it is about adapting, growing, and thriving despite life's challenges. It is the ability to bounce back from setbacks, to learn from difficult experiences, and to emerge stronger on the other side. Resilience turns obstacles into opportunities and setbacks into steps towards success. It is about developing the inner strength to navigate life's inevitable difficulties. The Bible reminds us that our strength comes from God, and by aligning our actions with His Word, we can face life's challenges with grace and perseverance.

I learned this firsthand when my life took an unexpected turn. My spouse has received a diagnosis of ALS. My mother suffered a stroke. Overnight, I became a full-time caregiver, navigating a world I had no training for, making decisions I never thought I would have to make. It was not just a shift in responsibility; it was a complete transformation of my life.

I had to retire early, something for which I had not planned. I had to leave Atlanta, the place I called home, and move to Jacksonville to create a new space, one that was safe and accessible for my husband and mother. My days became filled with medical appointments, ALS therapy sessions, and learning how to adjust every aspect of our lives to meet their needs. Nothing was the same.

At first, it was overwhelming. The weight of it all felt crushing. I had moments where I questioned if I could manage it if I were strong enough, patient enough, or resilient enough. But in those moments of doubt, I remembered that resilience is not about having all the answers or feeling completely in control. It is about adapting. It is about showing up, even when you do not feel ready. It is about accepting what you cannot change, focusing on what you can, and finding strength in your faith.

There were days I felt drained, unseen, and exhausted beyond words. But I also found something unexpected on this journey: a deeper strength, a capacity to endure, and a perspective on life that I never would have gained otherwise. I learned to embrace each day as it comes, to find joy in small victories, and to trust that God had given me this role for a reason.

This experience taught me that resilience is not just about enduring hardship; it's about transforming through it. While we cannot always control what happens to us, we can control how we react. Caregiving changed me in ways I never expected, but it also gave me a deeper understanding of what it truly means to be strong.

If you are facing a challenge that feels insurmountable, remember this: You are stronger than you think. Every obstacle is an opportunity to gain experience, and every hardship shapes you into someone more resilient. It may not be easy, but it will be worth it.

Developing a Resilient Mindset

Resilience is a skill we can cultivate. It involves several key components, including acceptance, optimism, self-efficacy (belief in your ability to succeed), and strong social support. The following strategies have been instrumental in my journey, and I hope they will empower you as well.

The Power of Words

Proverbs 18:21 tells us, *"The tongue has the power of life and death."* What we say, both to ourselves and to others, holds immense power. Positive affirmations rooted in truth can transform our perspective and strengthen our resolve.

- *"I am fearfully and wonderfully made"* (Psalm 139:14).

- *"I can do all things through Christ who strengthens me"* (Philippians 4:13).

- *"God has not given me a spirit of fear, but of power, love, and a sound mind"* (2 Timothy 1:7).

Action Item: Write three affirmations based on Scripture that align with your current challenges. For example, if you are struggling with feeling overwhelmed, you might write, *"I cast all my anxiety on Him because He cares for me"* (1 Peter 5:7). Speak these aloud each morning and evening, declaring God's truth over your life.

Visualization Techniques

The Bible urges us to fix our minds on what is right and true.

Philippians 4:8 says, *"Whatever is true, whatever is noble, whatever is right, whatever is pure, think about such things."*

Visualization allows us to focus on God's promises and envision His faithfulness as we navigate challenges.

Guided Exercise:

1. Consider a present issue you are encountering. Close your eyes and visualize God equipping you with the strength to overcome it.

2. Picture yourself walking boldly in His purpose, surrounded by His peace and provision.

3. End with a prayer of gratitude for His guidance.

Briefly describe your vision below:

_____

_____

_____

Reframing Negative Thoughts

Romans 12:2 teaches us to *"be transformed by the renewing of your mind."* Cognitive Behavioral Therapy (CBT) mirrors this principle by encouraging us to replace negative thoughts with God's truth.

Example:

- **Negative thought:** "I can't manage this."

- **Biblical truth:** *"God is my refuge and strength, an ever-present help in trouble"* (Psalm 46:1). And *"I can do all things through Christ who strengthens me"* (Philippians 4:13).

- **Reframed Thought:** "I can manage this quickly and with ease. God is my strength, and He is ever present with me. I do all things through Christ who strengthens me."

Action Item: Write down one negative thought with which you have been struggling. Then, find a Bible verse that counters it, write it out, and meditate on that truth throughout the week.

_____

_____

_____

Emotional Intelligence

Emotional intelligence plays a crucial role in building resilience. It involves understanding and managing your own emotions, as well as empathizing with others.

- **Self-Awareness:** Psalm 139:23 says, *"Search me, God, and know my heart; test me and know my anxious thoughts."* Self-awareness begins with inviting God to reveal what is within us. Journaling is a practical way to reflect on how our emotions influence our behavior. Understanding your emotional triggers allows you to respond more effectively to challenging situations.

- **Empathy:** Jesus modeled perfect empathy, stepping into our world and bearing our burdens. Galatians 6:2 says, *"Carry each other's burdens, and in this way, you will fulfill the law of Christ."* Practicing empathy allows us to connect with others, offer support, and build stronger relationships, which are vital for resilience.

- **Self-Regulation:** Proverbs 16:32 teaches, *"Better a patient person than a warrior, one with self-control than one who takes a city."* Managing our emotions with wisdom and patience allows us to respond thoughtfully instead of reacting impulsively. Self-regulation helps us avoid making rash decisions in stressful situations and enables us to maintain a sense of calm.

Strengthening Social Support

Ecclesiastes 4:9-10 reminds us, *"Two are better than one because they have a good return for their labor: If either of them falls down, one can help the other up."* Nurturing relationships with family, friends, and fellow believers is vital for resilience. Social support provides us with emotional, practical, and informational assistance during challenging times.

- **Building a Strong Support System:** Cultivate relationships with people who uplift and encourage you. Be open about your struggles and be willing to ask for help when needed. Do not hesitate to lean on your support network during challenging times.

- **Seeking Professional Help:** The Bible shows us the value of wise counsel. Proverbs 15:22 says, *"Plans fail for lack of counsel, but with many advisers they succeed."* Seeking therapy or counseling is a step of strength and wisdom, aligning with God's provision through others. It is a sign of self-awareness and a commitment to personal growth.

- **Joining Support Groups:** Matthew 18:20 promises, *"For where two or three gather in my name, there am I with them."* Being part of a community that shares your faith and the burden of your challenges will provide strength and comfort. Support groups offer a safe space to share experiences, learn coping strategies, and receive encouragement from others who understand.

The Importance of Sleep

Sleep is a gift from God, essential for restoring our bodies and minds. Psalm 127:2 says, *"He grants sleep to those He loves."* Prioritizing rest allows us to face challenges with clarity and strength. Lack of sleep can impair our judgment, increase irritability, and make it harder to cope with stress.

Practical Tip: Create a bedtime routine that includes prayer or reading Scripture to calm your mind and prepare your spirit for restful sleep. Aim for 7-9 hours of quality sleep each night.

Additional Ways to Encourage Peaceful Sleep:
• Sip herbal teas like chamomile or Sleepy Time tea an hour before bed
• Use a lavender or eucalyptus spray on your pillow for relaxation
• Turn off screens at least 30 minutes before bedtime
• Practice deep breathing or guided relaxation prayers
• Listen to calming instrumental worship music or audio Bible verses
• Dim the lights to signal your body that it's time to rest
• Keep your bedroom cool, dark, and quiet to promote deep sleep

Resting is essential, not selfish.

Reflection Journal

- Describe a current challenge you are facing.

_____

_____

_____

- What are your initial emotional responses to this challenge?

_____

_____

_____

- What are some positive affirmations or Bible verses that can help you reframe your thinking?

_____

_____

_____

- What specific steps can you take to address this challenge? Focus on what you can control.

_____

_____

_____

- Who can you reach out to for support and encouragement? What will you ask them?

- How can you practice self-care during this time to maintain your emotional and physical well-being?

- Reflect on how God might be using this challenge to grow you and strengthen your resilience.

SMART Goal:

- **Specific:** I will strengthen my mental resilience by reaching out to one supportive person each week to reflect, share, or pray.

- **Measurable:** One meaningful connection each week for 4 weeks.

- **Achievable:** A phone call, coffee, or message is realistic and doable.

- **Relevant:** Talking to people who have supported me will help reinforce resilience and reduce self-doubt.

- **Time Bound:** Perform this task once a week for the next four weeks.

Now it is your turn. Set your own SMART goal below:

S – Specific:

_____

_____

M – Measurable:

_____

_____

A – Achievable:

_____

_____

R – Relevant:

_____

_____

T – Time-bound:

_____

_____

Prayer:

Dear Heavenly Father:

Lord, I come before you seeking strength and guidance as I navigate the challenges in my life. Thank you for the promise that You are always with me, even during the storm. Please help me cultivate the qualities of resilience: acceptance, optimism, and faith. Please grant me the wisdom to discern what I can control and the courage to let go of what I cannot. Surround me with Your peace and equip me with the strength to face each day with hope and confidence. I pray these experiences draw me closer to you and make me stronger and more resilient.

In Jesus' name, Amen.

Closing Thoughts

Building resilience is a journey, not a destination. Be patient with yourself, celebrate small victories, and remember that God is always with you, guiding and supporting you every step of the way. You are stronger than you think.

DATE: _____

DATE: _____

Chapter 13

Adapting to Challenges

Ecclesiastes 3:1 (NIV) *"There is a time for everything, and a season for every activity under the heavens."*

Life is a journey of constant change, marked by transitions at every milestone. Like the shifting seasons, each phase of life challenges us to grow, stretch, and adapt. From high school to college, entering the workforce, navigating career shifts, or stepping into retirement, change demands resilience, humility, and faith.

Many people think they are prepared to manage change, but when they confront it directly, the reality often feels different. Adapting is not just about surviving; it is about finding purpose, peace, and growth through each transition.

Consider Ava, a high school senior preparing for college. Ava is ambitious and determined, but her family's financial struggles make the transition daunting. Scholarships, part-time work, and mounting responsibilities weigh heavily on her. She told me, "How will I make this work when everything feels like an uphill battle?" Ava's story reminds us that adaptability is essential, even at an early age.

Understanding Adaptation

Adaptation is the process of adjusting to new realities, challenges, or life seasons with grace, resilience, and purpose. It requires letting go of what was and embracing what is, often without having all the answers.

Spiritually, adaptation is an act of trust. It means surrendering our plans and expectations to God, believing He is working all things together for our good (Romans 8:28). Emotionally and mentally, it calls us to stay flexible, to shift our mindset, and to build new rhythms that reflect our current needs and responsibilities.

Adaptation is not about weakness but about wisdom. It is the ability to realign with God's will, remain steady during uncertainty, and move forward with intentional faith, even when the path looks different from what we imagined.

Adaptation Example: Nova's Reflection

A common challenge many individuals face is learning to seek assistance, particularly when accustomed to being the resilient one. For me, adaptation has meant shifting from trying to manage everything on my own to intentionally building a support system on which I can rely.

This week, I am choosing to:
• Delegate tasks that do not require my direct attention
• Set aside intentional time for rest and personal reflection
• Release guilt and receive grace as I grow through this season.

Adaptation does not always require a complete life overhaul. It begins with honest awareness of what is no longer sustainable, a renewed mindset, and small, intentional steps that align with your current season of life. Who can you reach out to for support and encouragement? Set a specific time or reminder to connect.

What advice did I give Ava that helped her adapt and overcome?

I informed Ava that strength is cultivated through the gradual process of decision-making, rather than possessing complete knowledge from the outset. I encouraged her to focus on what *is* within her control: applying for every scholarship available, building a realistic budget, and creating a weekly schedule that balances work and study. Most importantly, I told her to give herself permission to rest and ask for help when needed. We also prayed together, asking God to open doors no one else could shut. I told her, "You do not have to climb the whole mountain today, just take the next faithful step. That is how innovations happen.

Then there's Jane, a recent college graduate entering the workforce. Jane believed her degree was the key to immediate success, expecting to land a six-figure job right out of school. However, her applications for every position have been unsuccessful. Frustrated and disillusioned, she shared, "I thought college was the answer, but no one told me it would be this hard to get started." For Jane, adapting meant redefining her expectations and finding new ways to grow professionally.

Finally, consider Jim, a retiree at 67. After an extraordinarily successful career, Jim retired financially and was in excellent health. Yet, during our coaching sessions, Jim revealed he was struggling with depression. He said, "I don't know who Jim is anymore." For many years, his identity was his work, and the absence of it left him feeling disoriented, without purpose and identity.

These stories highlight a universal truth: no matter the stage of life, adapting to change requires humility, preparation, and reliance on God.

The Biblical Perspective on Change

While change can feel overwhelming, Scripture assures us that God is always at work, even in the most uncertain times. Isaiah 43:19 declares, *"See, I am doing a new thing! Now it springs up; do you not perceive it? I am making a way in the wilderness and streams in the wasteland."*

Change often feels like a wilderness, uncertain and disorienting. But God's promise is clear: He will create streams of provision, clarity, and renewal amid it all. Trusting in His plan gives us the courage to embrace change with faith.

The Role of Humility in Adapting

Adapting to change requires humility, the ability to admit that we don't have all the answers, and acknowledging the need for God's guidance. Proverbs 3:5-6 reminds us, *"Trust in the Lord with all your heart and lean not on your own understanding; in all your ways submit to Him, and He will make your paths straight."*

Humility allows us to release control and seek God's wisdom. Whether Ava relies on her family's support, Jane rethinks her career path, or Jim seeks a new sense of purpose, humility paves the way for growth and transformation.

The Power of Gratitude Journaling

Gratitude shifts our perspective, helping us focus on what we have rather than what we lack. 1 Thessalonians 5:18 encourages us to *"Give thanks in all circumstances; for this is God's will for you in Christ Jesus."*

Gratitude journaling is a simple yet transformative practice. Writing down blessings, big or small, creates an awareness of God's faithfulness, even during times of change, conflict, and challenge. Journal things that you are grateful for and things for which you are thankful.

_____

_____

_____

The Importance of Self-Care

Self-care is not indulgent; it is essential. Taking care of your body, mind, and spirit equips you to manage challenges with clarity and strength. 1 Corinthians 6:19-20 reminds us, *"Do you not know that your bodies are temples of the Holy Spirit... Therefore, honor God with your bodies."*

The Role of Community

Community is one of God's greatest gifts during seasons of change.

Ecclesiastes 4:9-10 says, *"Two are better than one because they have a good return for their labor: If either of them falls down, one can help the other up."* A strong community offers encouragement, accountability, and prayer support. Surround yourself with people who reflect God's love and uplift you during transitions.

Guardrails for Handling Challenges: Understanding HALT

HALT: Hungry, Angry, Lonely, Tired.

When adapting to challenges, recognizing your emotional and physical state is critical. A powerful tool to keep in mind is HALT: Hungry, Angry, Lonely, Tired. These conditions can cloud judgment, increase impulsivity, and make it harder to navigate challenges effectively. For example, attempting to have a difficult conversation when you are tired or angry can lead to unnecessary conflict. HALT encourages us to pause, assess, and address these needs before making decisions. In the military, the command halt means to stop. When given this command, the unit will stop and stay in place until another command is given. Guardrails and boundaries help us to stop and evaluate before moving forward.

Practical Guardrails

- **Pause Before Reacting:** If you recognize you are in a HALT state, address it before responding or making a critical decision.

- **Refuel with Gratitude:** Reflect on blessings to reset your mindset.

- **Seek Rest and Prayer:** Take time to restore your energy and seek God's wisdom before moving forward.

Think about a time in your life when you demonstrated adaptation. What strengths did you draw upon? What did you learn from the experience? How has that experience shaped you into the person you are today?

Reflection Journal

What is one specific change or challenge you are currently facing or anticipating?

_____

_____

_____

- What are your initial thoughts and feelings about this change, and how are those affecting your ability to adapt?

_____

_____

_____

- How can you cultivate humility and lean on God's guidance as you navigate this transition?

_____

_____

_____

- What are some practical self-care strategies you can implement to support your well-being during this time of change?

_____

_____

_____

- Who are the people in your life who can offer support and encouragement, and how can you reach out to them?

_____

_____

_____

- How can you use the HALT principle to set guardrails and ensure you approach challenges with a clear and grounded perspective?

_____

_____

_____

- What are some specific blessings you can focus on and express gratitude for, even amidst the challenges of this transition? What can you be thankful for in this current challenge?

_____

_____

SMART Goal:

- **Specific:** I want to grow in my ability to adapt by creating space to process and pray through the change I am currently facing.

- **Measurable:** I will do this 5 days a week for the next 3 weeks.

- **Achievable:** Setting aside 15 minutes each evening fits into my current schedule,

- **Relevant:** This will help me strengthen my ability to adapt with clarity, humility, and trust in God.

- **Time-Bound:** I will begin today and continue consistently for 3 weeks.

Now it is your turn. Set your own SMART goal below:

S – Specific:

_____

_____

M – Measurable:

_____

_____

A – Achievable:

_____

_____

R – Relevant:

_____

_____

T – Time-bound:

_____

_____

Prayer

Dear Heavenly Father:

Lord, grant me the strength and resilience to adapt to the changes in my life. Help me to embrace transitions with a humble heart, seeking Your wisdom and guidance. Fill me with gratitude for Your constant presence and provision, even in uncertain times. Surround me with a supportive community and empower me to practice self-care. Teach me to recognize my emotional and physical needs, setting healthy guardrails as I navigate challenges. May I emerge from each transition stronger and more aligned with Your purpose for my life.

In Jesus' name, Amen.

Closing Thoughts

Adapting to challenges is a process of growth, faith, and intentionality. It requires humility to seek God's guidance, gratitude to shift your perspective, self-care to nurture your strength, and community to walk alongside you, as well as the ability to change. By embracing these principles, you can navigate life's transitions with confidence, knowing that God is with you every step of the way.

DATE: _____

DATE: _____

Chapter 14

Navigating Life Transitions, Embracing Change

Proverbs 16:9 (NIV): *"In their hearts humans plan their course, but the Lord establishes their steps."*

Life is a journey marked by transitions, each one a new chapter in our story. Whether it is a career change, moving to a new city, or navigating a significant life event, transitions can be both exciting and challenging. The key to navigating these seasons is embracing them with faith, resilience, and intentionality, trusting that even when our plans shift, God is faithfully ordering our steps.

The Biblical Perspective on Change

Change is part of life. Like nature's seasons, our lives have phases of growth, harvest, and rest. Each season brings its own set of challenges and opportunities, requiring us to adapt and grow. While change can feel unsettling, Scripture offers constant reassurance that God is sovereign.

Isaiah 43:19 declares, *"See, I am doing a new thing! Now it springs up; do you not perceive it? I am making my way in the wilderness and streams in the wasteland."* This verse reminds us that God is not only aware of the changes we face, but also actively involved in shaping them for our good.

Even when we find ourselves in a metaphorical wilderness, feeling lost and disoriented, God promises to provide a way forward, creating streams of provision, clarity, and renewal. Remember that Romans 8:28 states, *"That all things work together for good to those who love God and are called according to his purpose."*

Embracing Change with Faith, Patience, and Mindfulness

Navigating transitions with grace requires steadfast faith in God's plan. Hebrews 11:1 defines faith as *"confidence in what we hope for and assurance about what we do not see."* When we place our trust in God, we can face the unknown with courage, knowing that He is in control and that His plans for us are good.

Patience is another essential virtue during times of transition. James 1:4 teaches, *"Let perseverance finish its work so that you may be mature and complete, not lacking anything."* Transitions often require time and can test our patience. However, by trusting in God's timing and allowing perseverance to do its work in us, we can grow in maturity and completeness.

Mindfulness practices, such as meditation, deep breathing, or Scripture-focused reflection, can help us stay grounded and present during times of change. By focusing on the present moment, we can reduce anxiety, gain clarity, and cultivate a sense of peace amidst the uncertainties of transition.

Mindfulness is about intentionally paying attention to the present moment without judgment. Observe your thoughts, feelings, and sensations without succumbing to them. This practice allows you to create space between your reactions and your responses, enabling you to make the best possible conscious choices.

The Power of Gratitude and Self-Care in Transitions

Gratitude has the power to transform our perspective during transitions. 1 Thessalonians 5:18 reminds us, *"Give thanks in all circumstances; for this is God's will for you in Christ Jesus."* Even during change and uncertainty, there is always something for which to be grateful. Developing a mindset of gratitude enables us to concentrate on the positive aspects, enhance our resilience, and discover peace during challenging times.

Self-care is equally crucial during life transitions. Prioritizing your physical, emotional, and spiritual well-being equips you to manage the challenges and stresses that often accompany change. Self-care stewardship involves recognizing the importance of nurturing and resting your mind and body.

The Importance of Setting Boundaries

Transitions often bring additional demands on our time, energy, and emotions. Setting healthy boundaries is essential for protecting your well-being and ensuring that you can navigate change effectively. Boundaries are about recognizing your limits and communicating them clearly to others. They are about saying "no" to things that drain you and "yes" to things that nourish your soul.

Jesus himself modeled the importance of setting boundaries. In Luke 5:16, we read that *"Jesus often withdrew to lonely places and prayed.*" Even amidst the demands of His ministry, Jesus recognized the need for solitude and time with the Father. By setting boundaries, you create space for rest, reflection, and spiritual renewal, enabling you to navigate transitions with clarity and strength.

The Role of Community in Transitions

Transitions may be isolating, but we are not meant to go through them alone. Proverbs 27:17 reminds us, *"As iron sharpens iron, so one person sharpens another."* The community provides a vital source of support, encouragement, and wisdom during life's changes. You can navigate successfully by surrounding yourself with people who uplift you, share your values, and offer honest feedback. People who will hold you accountable and responsible for your actions with love and compassion.

Reflection Journal

- What is one significant life transition you are currently experiencing or anticipating?

_____

_____

_____

- What are the biggest challenges you are facing or expect to face during this transition?

_____

- How can you actively cultivate faith and trust in God's plan as you navigate this change?

- What specific mindfulness practices can you incorporate into your daily routine to stay grounded and present during this transition?

- What are you grateful for in this season, even amidst the challenges of change? How can you express your gratitude and thanksgiving more intentionally?

- What self-care practices can you prioritize to nurture your physical, emotional, and spiritual well-being during this time of transition?

- What boundaries do you need to set to protect your time, energy, and emotional health during this transition?

_____

_____

_____

- Who are the people in your life who can offer support, encouragement, and accountability as you navigate this change? How can you actively engage with them?

_____

_____

_____

SMART Goal:

- **Specific:** I am transitioning into a new caregiver role, and I want to establish a daily rhythm that allows me to care for my loved ones while also maintaining my own well-being.

- **Measurable:** I will track my progress by creating a weekly schedule and journaling once a week to reflect on what is working and what needs adjusting.

- **Achievable:** I will start with small daily anchors, morning prayers, 15-minute breaks, and a bedtime routine that is realistic and sustainable in this season.

- **Relevant:** The goal supports both my responsibility as a caregiver and my personal values of peace, balance, and intentional living.

- **Time-Bound:** Over the next 30 days, I will implement and adjust this rhythm to create a sustainable routine that supports both the transition and my well-being.

Now it is your turn. Set your own SMART goal below:

S – Specific:

_____

_____

M – Measurable:

_____

_____

A – Achievable:

_____

_____

R – Relevant:

_____

_____

T – Time-bound:

_____

_____

Prayer

Dear Heavenly Father:

Lord, guide me as I navigate the transitions in my life. Grant me the faith to trust Your plan, the patience to wait on Your timing, and the mindfulness to stay present in each moment. Fill my heart with gratitude for Your blessings and empower me to prioritize self-care. Give me Your wisdom to set healthy boundaries and surround me with a supportive community. May I embrace change with confidence, knowing that You are with me every step of the way.

In Jesus' name, Amen.

Closing Thoughts

Navigating life's transitions requires faith, patience, and intentionality. By trusting in God's plan, practicing gratitude, setting boundaries, and leaning on your community, you can emerge stronger, more resilient, and closer to fulfilling His purpose.

DATE: _____

DATE: _____

Chapter 15

The Power of Community: Love in Action

1 John 3:18 (NIV) *"Dear children, let us not love with words or speech but with actions in truth."*

A strong community is not just about the people who live around you; it is about the support, love, and strength that bind us together. It is about being there for one another, not just in words but in action. The Bible is clear about the importance of community, calling us to love our neighbors, serve one another, and carry each other's burdens.

I have always believed in giving back. I have volunteered in various capacities throughout my life, including aiding people experiencing homelessness, rescuing animals, and supporting causes that hold a special place in my heart. One of the most fulfilling ways I have served was teaching a ninth-grade Sunday school class for four years. Pouring into young minds, helping them grow in faith, and guiding them through those critical years was a blessing for me. The church has always been a core part of my life, and serving in this way deepened my understanding of what a true community looks like.

Being a servant leader has always been a guiding principle for me. The strength and resilience of our community were evident following my spouse's diagnosis of ALS. That moment knocked us off our feet. That was when our community stepped in.

The Biblical Importance of Community

Community is God's design. He never intended for us to walk through life alone. Scripture repeatedly reminds us of the power of relationships and the need to serve and support one another.

• Love Thy Neighbor – *"Love your neighbor as yourself."* (Mark 12:31). This is more than just a command; it is a way of life. Loving your neighbor is not just about words; it is about action. It means being there in times of need, stepping up, and showing kindness when it matters most.

• Bearing One Another's Burdens – *"Carry each other's burdens, and in this way, you will fulfill the law of Christ."* (Galatians 6:2). We are not meant to struggle alone. Our friends and neighbors can be a strong community that is strong for us when we feel weak.

• The Power of Fellowship– *"For where two or three are gathered in My name, there am I among them."* (Matthew 18:20). God moves in community. Community bonds thrive through gathering, collaboration, and mutual support.

• The Principle of Reciprocity – *"Give, and it will be given to you. A fair portion, fully measured and overflowing, will be given to you."* (Luke 6:38) What we pour into others, we will see returned in ways we never expected.

Our Community Showed Up for Us

We moved from Georgia to Jacksonville to be closer to my family during this time. With my mother having a stroke and my husband battling ALS, I knew relocating was the right decision, but I had no idea just how incredible the people around us would be.

When the moving trucks arrived, thirteen amazing people showed up at my house. They did not just help unload; they put my entire home together, decorated it, and made sure everything felt like I had lived there forever. Their kindness and generosity left me indebted to them for life. They were the right neighbors for us at that time and stage in our lives, and that matters immensely.

Be aware of when you can be that neighbor for someone else.

Beyond that, our work family at DIRECTV organized a meal train, checked on us constantly, sent gifts, and stood by us during this challenging time. People whom I never expected to step up were suddenly lifelines for us. Neighbors we had barely known started showing up, dropping off food and blankets, offering their time, energy, and love.

And then, there was our church family. They prayed for us, walked alongside us, and reminded us that God's love shines brightest through His people.

Through every hardship, I have learned this: We are not as strong as we think we are— we need our community to help us shoulder the load and support one another.

Reflection Journal

• What specific ways can you step up and serve others in your neighborhood, workplace, or church?

_____

_____

_____

• What factors hinder community engagement, and what methods can be used to address them?

_____

_____

_____

• Reflect on a time when you felt God was working through others to bless you.

_____

_____

_____

Write down one way you will actively invest in your community this week:

_____

_____

_____

SMART Goal:

- **Specific** – I will give back to my community by volunteering or tangibly serving others.

- **Measurable** – I will volunteer 2 hours per week supporting a community outreach

- **Achievable** – I will start with one simple act each week, such as preparing a meal for someone in need.

- **Relevant** – This goal reflects my desire to live out my faith through serving others.

- **Time-bound** – I will consistently serve for 2 hours per week over the next 6 weeks and reflect on how it has impacted both others and me.

Now it is your turn. Set your own SMART goal below:

S – Specific:

_____

_____

M – Measurable:

_____

_____

A – Achievable:

_____

_____

R – Relevant:

_____

_____

T – Time-bound:

_____

_____

Prayer

Heavenly Father,

Thank you for the gift of the community. You have designed us to walk together, to lift one another, and to reflect Your love through our actions. Lord, I ask that You strengthen the bonds within my community. Help me to see where I can serve, where I can encourage, and where I can have influence. Give me the wisdom to love my neighbor as myself, to bear the burdens of others, and to be a light in the darkness.

May my actions glorify You, and may my service bring hope to those in need. I trust that as I give, You will provide, and as I love, You will fill me with even greater love.

In Jesus' name, Amen.

Closing Thoughts

Community is everything. It provides support when we are unable to stand alone. It is love in action, faith in motion, and hope in a tangible form. When we invest in those around us, we create a ripple effect of kindness and generosity.

We will all face hardships. It is not a matter of 'if' but 'when'. This underscores the significance of the community, as we all will require assistance at some point in time. If you are healthy, give back while you have the ability. Serve. Support. Encourage. If you are financially secure, give to the needs of others.

Do not just say you love your neighbor, show it. Help them, walk alongside them, and be present in their struggles. We should help others and show compassion through meaningful actions. Paying it forward and taking care of one another make life more bearable, meaningful, and beautiful.

So today, I encourage you: Be the neighbor, be the friend, be the family someone needs. And when your time comes, your community will be there for you, just as God intended.

DATE: _____

DATE: _____

Chapter 16

The Blessing of Healed and Restored Emotions

Psalm 147:3 (NIV) *"He heals the brokenhearted and binds up their wounds."*

Emotions are a powerful gift from God. Understanding and addressing them is essential. Just like physical wounds need cleansing and care to heal properly, emotional wounds require attention, truth, and surrender to God's healing hand.

Managing emotions like grief, anger, or anxiety is commonly recommended. We often receive advice to persevere or remain resilient, even in times of internal struggle. But suppressed emotions do not disappear; they simply go underground and resurface as bitterness, burnout, or breakdown. Emotional healing begins when we stop pretending that we are fine and acknowledge our truth.

When we allow God into our pain, He transforms it. He helps us see the roots, forgive where necessary, and walk in peace again.

A Story of Sabotage: How Unhealed Emotions Steal Our Future

I once coached a woman named Shari, who was incredibly talented, bright, driven, and positioned for leadership in her company. Yet every promotion she chased seemed to fall apart at the last minute. After some prayer and deep reflection, she shared something that shifted everything: "Every time I feel overlooked, I go into defense mode. I started pulling away. I tell myself they do not value me, and I begin looking for flaws in everyone else instead of addressing my own insecurities."

Shari did not realize it, but her unhealed wounds from past rejection were sabotaging her present success. She had experienced deep abandonment in childhood and had never allowed herself to deal with that pain fully. She responded with perfectionism and emotional distance, rather than acknowledgment. But her co-workers and leaders could feel her guardedness. They could not connect with her, and trust could not grow.

Similarly, I have seen people sabotage marriages, friendships, and divine assignments because of unchecked emotional triggers. One individual ended a relationship due to concerns over potential harm, like what his father caused his mother. Anytime his girlfriend showed concern or asked questions, he interpreted it as control. His past distorted his present, and without healing, he kept repeating the same pattern in every relationship.

Emotional healing is not optional; it is essential. If we do not address our emotional pain, we will bleed on people who never cut us.

What Healing Looks Like

Healed emotions help you:

- Respond instead of reacting.

- Forgive rather than hold grudges.

- Set healthy boundaries instead of building walls.

- Speak truth with grace instead of silence or sharpness!

- Walk in peace instead of panicking.

God does not ask us to heal alone. He invites us into a relationship where we can be honest, raw, and real. He gently reveals the roots of our pain and provides the strength to forgive, release, and rebuild.

Healing Happens in the Community

God often uses safe people to be part of our healing. A mentor, friend, counselor, or pastor can offer perspective and prayer. Just as the body has many parts, emotional wholeness requires connection. 1 Corinthians 12:21-22 says, *"The eye cannot say to the hand, 'I don't need you!' And the head cannot say to the feet, 'I don't need you!' On the contrary, those parts of the body that are weaker are indispensable."*

You were never meant to heal in isolation. Whether through professional help or prayerful support, God works through others to bring restoration.

Reflection Journal

What emotions do I tend to suppress or ignore?

_____

_____

_____

How have unhealed emotions affected my decisions or relationships?

_____

_____

_____

What would emotional freedom look like in my life?

_____

_____

SMART Goal

- Specific: Identify one dominant emotion that feels unresolved (e.g., fear, resentment).

- Measurable: Spend 15 minutes three times this week in prayer or journaling about that emotion.

- Achievable: Choose one action step: schedule a counseling session, talk to a mentor, or write a forgiveness letter (even if not sent).

- Relevant: Emotional healing leads to stronger relationships and spiritual freedom.

- Time-Bound: Begin this week and commit to the process for the next 14 days.

Now it is your turn. Set your own SMART goal below:

S – Specific:

_____

_____

M – Measurable:

_____

_____

A – Achievable:

_____

_____

R – Relevant:

_____

_____

T – Time-bound:

_____

_____

Prayer

Heavenly Father,

I bring You the parts of me that still feel broken. I bring the pain I have buried, the emotions I have avoided, and the fears I have carried. Lord, I no longer want these wounds to shape my choices or my future. I ask You to search my heart and heal what hurts. Help me release unforgiveness, fear, and grief. Please fill me with peace, clarity, and emotional resilience. Give me wisdom to recognize my patterns and courage to respond in a new way. I trust you to repair what is broken inside of me.

In Jesus' name, Amen.

Closing Thoughts

Emotional healing is rarely instant. It is a journey that unfolds with honesty, grace, and God's steady hands. When we bring our pain, grief, or buried emotions into the light, we permit God to do what only he can: heal the brokenhearted and bind up the wounds we have hidden.

DATE: _____

DATE: _____

Chapter 17

The Importance of Authentic Leadership in Personal Branding

Proverbs 22:1 (NIV) "A good name is more desirable than great riches; to be esteemed is better than silver or gold."

Authentic leadership means being genuine, consistent, and aligned with your values. Your brand encompasses more than just your outward appearance; it represents the essence of who you are. Whether you are a teenager building your future, a young professional shaping your career, or someone redefining your legacy, authenticity is your most significant asset.

As I have always told my children, the values and character you cultivate within yourself will inevitably influence how you interact with the world. Being authentic in your daily life ensures that your true self shines through in every aspect of life.

Bill Morrow, former CEO of DIRECTV, once said, "Be better today than you were yesterday." This resonated deeply with me and became my daily mantra. Every morning, I ask myself: "What are three key things I can do today to be better than I was yesterday?" This practice has helped me continuously build my skills mentally, emotionally, physically, spiritually, and financially.

List three things that you can begin to do better today than you did yesterday.

_____

_____

_____

Key Components of Personal Branding

1. Internal Values and Character:

Your core values, beliefs, and character traits influence your public persona and how you interact with the world. This is the bedrock of your brand. Without a solid foundation of integrity, authenticity, and self-awareness, the other components will lack substance. Your relationship with God is the foundation of who you are. Your God-given identity, knowing who God says you are, and knowing who God says He is, is critically important to your personal branding.

2. Your Professional Identity:

Your work ethic, communication, and leadership define how others perceive you professionally. This is how your internal values manifest in your career.

3. Your Community Engagement:

How you serve and connect with your community reflects your values and authenticity. This demonstrates your values in action beyond the workplace.

4. Your Digital Presence:

Every post, comment, and interaction on social media contributes to your personal brand. Your online behavior should be a consistent reflection of your core values.

5. **Resumes, Bios, and Building Your Brand Offline:**

Your personal brand extends beyond social media; it lives in your resume, bio, and everyday interactions.

• Resume: Your resume is not just a list of jobs; it is a marketing document that communicates your value.

• Use keywords relevant to your industry and brand.

• Quantify your achievements whenever possible.

• Highlight projects that demonstrate your unique skills and passions.

• Bio: Your bio is your first impression.

• Start with a strong hook that captures attention.

• Clearly articulate your value proposition.

• Include a call to action (e.g., connect to LinkedIn, visit your website).

• Everyday interactions:

Whether it's an email, a meeting, or a casual conversation, your communication style contributes to your personal brand. Be mindful of how you present yourself.

Understanding the Social Media Landscape

The digital world offers numerous platforms to cultivate your personal brand. Each platform serves a different purpose, and understanding their nuances is key:

• LinkedIn: Optimize your profile, engage in industry discussions, and connect with professionals.

• Twitter: Share insights and news, and establish yourself as a thought leader.

• Instagram: Highlight your personality and passions visually.

• Facebook: Share updates, engage in discussions, and build relationships.

• YouTube: Create valuable content that resonates with your target audience.

Digital Footprint Warning:

What you post online lives forever. Be mindful. Before posting, ask yourself, "Would I be okay if my future employer, family, or church saw this?" Your digital footprint can either build your personal brand or tarnish it.

Steps to Build an Authentic Personal Brand

1. Identify Your Authentic Self: Reflect on your values, passions, and strengths.

2. Define Your Target Audience: Who are you trying to reach?

3. Craft Your Brand Message: What key message do you want to convey?

4. Develop Your Brand Assets: Resume, bio, website, and social media.

5. Build Your Network: Connect with like-minded individuals.

6. Be Consistent: Maintain a consistent brand image and message.

7. Refine and Evolve: Continuously evaluate and refine your brand.

Practical Tools for Managing Your Personal Brand

• Canva: For creating visually appealing resumes, social media posts, and presentations.

• LinkedIn Learning: For courses on personal branding, leadership, and communication.

•Grammarly: For polished and professional writing.

• Google Alerts: To monitor mentions of your name online.

• Hootsuite: To manage and schedule social media posts.

• Time-bound: Set deadlines and review every 90 days.

• Professional Branding Services: Digital marketers and branding professionals can help you refine and enhance your personal brand. Investing in these services can provide expert guidance, help craft a compelling online presence, and ensure your brand aligns with your goals and values.

Crafting an Authentic Mission Statement

A mission statement is a concise declaration of your purpose and values.

Example: "To empower individuals to achieve their full potential through innovative coaching and training programs."

Living Authentically at Every Stage of Life

Transformation at Any Age is about building a foundation that allows you to navigate life's transitions with confidence. Your personal brand evolves with you, but its authenticity remains constant. Each milestone provides an opportunity to strengthen your brand.

For Teens: Build a positive digital footprint. What you post today can affect your future.

For Young Professionals: Network actively and continue learning.

For Mid-Career Individuals: Mentor others and refine your skills.

For Retirees: Share your wisdom, mentor, and stay active in your community.

Reflection Journal

What are your core values?

_____

_____

_____

What does your current personal brand say about you?

_____

_____

_____

What steps will you take to improve your personal brand?

_____

_____

_____

SMART Goal

• Specific: I will improve my personal brand by updating my LinkedIn profile to reflect my core values and leadership style.

• Measurable: I will update four key areas of my LinkedIn profile.

• Achievable: I will dedicate 30 minutes each week to focus on one section, which is manageable with my current schedule.

• Relevant: This goal supports my commitment to authentic leadership and ensures my digital presence aligns with who I am.

• Time-Bound: I will complete all updates within 4 weeks.

Now it is your turn. Set your own SMART goal below:

S – Specific:

_____

_____

M – Measurable:

_____

_____

A – Achievable:

_____

_____

R – Relevant:

_____

_____

T – Time-bound:

_____

_____

A Prayer

Dear Heavenly Father,

Thank You for guiding me in building an authentic personal brand. Please help me to stay true to my values, lead with integrity, and be a light to others. Let my actions reflect Your love and wisdom. Please grant me the courage to grow, the humility to learn, and the strength to serve others through every phase of life. Jesus, help me be the God person you created me to be.

In Jesus' name, Amen.

Closing Thoughts

Start today. Reflect on your values, identify your strengths, and align your online and offline presence with your true self. Update your LinkedIn profile, review your social media, and build your network with intention. Remember, your personal brand is your legacy; make it count.

DATE: _____

DATE: _____

Chapter 18

Lifelong Blueprint for Transformation

Philippians 4:13 (NIV) *"I can do all this through Christ who gives me strength."*

Transformation is not a one-time event; it is a lifelong commitment. In every phase of life, circumstances shift, challenges arise, and new opportunities emerge. To keep growing, you must continually reinvent yourself while reinforcing the foundation of the five pillars: spiritual, physical, mental, emotional, and financial. True transformation is about adapting, evolving, and staying intentional in your journey, no matter what season of life you are in.

Throughout this book, we have explored the key principles of transformation:

- Self-awareness – Understanding yourself, your strengths, and your blind spots.

- Resilience – Facing challenges head-on and adapting when necessary.

- Vision and Goal Setting – Mapping out a clear direction for your future. Remember to be flexible and open to changes in situations and circumstances.

- Accountability and Consistency - staying on track, adjusting when needed, and celebrating progress are crucial.

Now, it is time to bring everything together and commit to your own blueprint for lifelong transformation.

What Will Your Legacy Be?

What mark do you want to leave on the world? Imagine your grandchildren years from now, reflecting on your life. What story do you want them to tell? One of my own mental growth goals was to author a book not just for the sake of writing but to share my faith, inspire others, and leave a legacy of wisdom. I wanted to create something that would live beyond me, something that my grandchildren could look back on and say, "This is what my grandmother believed in. This is how she lived. This is what she stood for." More than that, my dream was to use my voice, my experiences, and my faith to help others grow in five key areas: spiritual, mental, emotional, physical, and financial. That dream started over a decade ago, and today, I am making it a reality.

But the transformation does not stop there. My blueprint has evolved as it should. I will have completed my PhD in Leadership and Theology, another crucial piece of my evolving blueprint, by the time this book is published. This allows me to deepen my understanding of faith and leadership, equipping me to guide others on their own journeys of transformation. My goal is to become an adjunct professor, helping the next generation develop as leaders in both faith and life.

What is *your* big goal? What dream have you been carrying for years but have not yet brought to life? It is never too late. As Ecclesiastes 3:1 says, *"There is a time for everything and a season for every activity under heaven."* Your season for transformation may be now.

Living the Blueprint Amid Life's Challenges

Life does stop us from pursuing our dreams. In fact, it frequently presents us with unexpected detours, roadblocks, and even storms. *"In their hearts, humans plan their course, but the Lord establishes their steps."* Proverbs 16:9. We can make plans, but we must trust that God's guidance will direct our paths.

Even as I pursue my vision, I am also navigating one of the most challenging transitions of my life. I am a caregiver to my husband and my mother. There are days when exhaustion sets in, when the emotional and physical toll feels overwhelming. There are moments when I want to crawl under the bed and hide from the weight of responsibility. Just last week, I had to make a difficult decision about my mother's care, which left me feeling emotionally drained.

But I do not stop. I go to God and seek to hear His voice. I trust Him, lean on His words, and seek the prayers and support of other believers. Because I follow my blueprint by being intentional and laser-focused, I balance my priorities. I manage my dashboard, constantly recalibrating, adjusting, and doing what I can without losing sight of my goals. I may not always move at full speed, but I never stop moving forward because I know that even small steps accumulate over time, and every step I take brings me closer to my vision. And I also know when to take quiet time and be at rest. *"Let us not become weary in doing good, for at the proper time, we will reap a harvest if we do not give up."* Galatians 6:9. My journey is proof that transformation is possible at any age.

Building Your Personal Blueprint

Your blueprint is your structured system designed to guide and transform you and keep you grounded, focused, and aligned with your values and goals. It is a personalized plan that outlines your vision, sets clear goals, and provides actionable steps to help you achieve lasting change in all areas of your life.

- **Define Your Vision & Make It Loud:** *"Where there is no vision, the people perish."* – Proverbs 29:18 (KJV). Your vision should be expansive, big, bold, and clear. It should reflect your deepest values and passions. Take time to prayerfully consider what truly matters to you, what impact you want to make, and what legacy you want to leave behind.

- **Cultivate Self-Awareness & Resilience:** *"For though a righteous person falls seven times, they rise again."* – Proverbs 24:16. One practical way to cultivate self-awareness is to journal regularly, reflecting on your thoughts, feelings, and actions. Ask yourself:

  - What are my strengths?

  - What areas do I need to improve?

- What triggers my negative emotions? Resilience is not about avoiding failure; it is about getting back up when you fall.

- **Set SMART Goals & Manage the Levers:** *"Write the vision; make it plain on tablets, so he may run who reads it."* – Habakkuk 2:2 (ESV). Let us say your goal is to improve your physical health. A SMART Goal might be: "I will walk for 30 minutes, three times a week, for the next 12 weeks." This is specific (walking), measurable (3 times a week), achievable (30 minutes is reasonable), relevant (to physical health), and time-bound (12 weeks).

- **Build an Accountability System:** *"As iron sharpens iron, so one person sharpens another."* – Proverbs 27:17 (NIV). Find an accountability partner, mentor, or support group who shares your values and goals. This could be a friend, a family member, a member of your church, or a professional coach. Discuss your blueprint with them and schedule regular check-ins to track your progress and stay motivated.

- **Celebrate Milestones & Keep Moving Forward:** *"Give thanks in all circumstances; for this is God's will for you in Christ Jesus."* – 1 Thessalonians 5:18. Even during challenges, gratitude helps us maintain perspective. We have all heard the phrase, never, never, never quit. Tap into the strength of scriptures, pray, and move forward with confidence that He is guiding you.

Your Call to Action: Start Today

So, I ask you: What is your big vision? What is one small, faith-filled step you can take today to move toward it? What areas of your life do you need to surrender to God's plan, trusting that He will establish your steps? If you do not create your own blueprint, life will create one for you. And I promise yours will be better. *"Commit to the Lord whatever you do, and he will establish your plans."* Proverbs 16:3. Start today. Please write it down. Make it clear. Manage the levers. Track your progress. And never stop transforming. Transformation is possible at any age. If I can do it, so can you.

Reflection Journal

Reflect on your journey through this book. What key insights resonated most with you?

_____

_____

_____

Where do you feel you have made progress, and where do you still want to grow?

_____

_____

_____

SMART Goal

- Specific: I will make a transformation plan from this book, setting one goal for each of the five pillars.
- Measurable: I will establish one specific goal for each pillar and monitor my progress through monthly self-assessments.
- Achievable: I will begin with small, realistic steps for each area to build momentum and avoid overwhelm.
- Relevant: This goal supports my commitment to personal growth and the values that I identified throughout this journey.
- Time-Bound: I will finalize my blueprint and begin implementation within the next 7 days, with a full review after 90 days.

Now it is your turn. Set your own SMART goal below:

S – Specific:

_____

_____

M – Measurable:

_____

_____

A – Achievable:

_____

_____

R – Relevant:

_____

_____

T – Time-bound:

_____

_____

Prayer

Dear Heavenly Father:

Thank You for the journey of transformation. Thank You for the lessons I have learned and the growth I have experienced. Enable me to continue pursuing my goals despite the challenges of caregiving and other life changes. Help me to trust in Your perfect timing and to find joy in the journey of transformation. I surrender my plans to You, knowing that You will guide my steps. Let my journey reflect Your grace and inspire others to seek You.

In Jesus' name, Amen.

Closing Thoughts

Transformation does not end with the last page; it begins again with every new decision you make. Your growth is not a one-time achievement, but a lifelong process, built day by day, choice by choice, and season by season. You now hold the tools, scriptures, and insights to build a life rooted in purpose, strength, and alignment. Keep refining. Keep Rising. And always remember you can do all thing through Christ who strengthens you.

DATE: _____

DATE: _____

Chapter 19

Your Journey Continues

Proverbs 13:22 (NIV) *"A good person leaves an inheritance for their children's children."*

Congratulations on completing this transformation journey. Stepping boldly into your next chapter, remember this fundamental truth: you are always under construction. Your life's foundation can be fragile or solid. When inevitable storms rage, only the structure crafted with care, intention, and unwavering strength will stand tall. The five essential pillars you have explored, spiritual, emotional, mental, physical, and financial, are the very bricks of a resilient life.

Keep your eyes fixed on your North Star, God's unique calling for your life. Establish firm daily boundaries. Clearly define your goals in writing or on a vision board. Relentlessly refine your focus. Surround yourself with individuals who challenge and elevate you, for as iron sharpens iron, so too does community foster growth, not isolation. Seek out mentors and, in turn, become a guiding light for others.

Always envision the outcome. As Brian Tracy wisely advises, reverse engineering your life. What level of health do you aspire to in retirement? What should your emotional and mental landscape look like? What is your desired net worth? Do you envision a debt-free life? What legacy do you wish to leave? These are examples of your strategic blueprints. Your daily habits and your unwavering discipline are the tactical steps that will pave the way.

Before you realize it, you will stand at the threshold of a new season. And you will want the bricks you have diligently laid to provide unwavering support and to sustain the legacy you will pass on. Proverbs 13:22 reminds us, *"A good person leaves an inheritance for their children's children."* Therefore, build with the end in mind. Build to endure.

My personal journey has been marked by deep loss and resilience. At just 14 years old, I faced the devastating tragedy of losing my father to suicide. That moment shattered my world and forced me to grow up quickly. In the years that followed, I encountered more challenges that could have defined me, but instead, they refined me. The path forward was anything but easy. These times were characterized by mistreatment, distress, apprehension, and uncertainty. Yet through it all, I learned that looking back can hold you back. God calls us to keep our eyes forward. Do not be like Lot's wife, who looked back and turned to a pillar of salt. (*"Forget the former things; do not dwell on the past."* Isaiah 43:18)

If your past has been rocky like mine, remember this: life is not perfect, and it never will be. However, by utilizing prayer, maintaining focus, and surrounding yourself with the right people, you can construct barriers and safeguard your journey. Continue to plant positive seeds in your garden, pull out the weeds of negativity, and celebrate every win. Love your family, cherish your neighbors, and embrace the beauty of life. And do not worry or fear, for God is with you every step of the way. (*"Do not worry about tomorrow, for tomorrow will worry about itself."* Matthew 6:34)

Through every phase of life, there is an opportunity to take what you have learned and help others. The most gratifying aspect of life is being a servant leader and being the light in this dark world. When you are in alignment physically, mentally, spiritually, and financially, your mental health thrives. You feel good, you sustain yourself, and you share your knowledge with others. As we mature and experience life's inevitable changes, we discover and impart valuable lessons from each stage of life as we help others grow on their transformational journey.

Nothing in life stands still. Everything evolves. Prepare yourself to navigate each milestone and celebrate it. Whether you are graduating from high school or heading to college, set ambitious goals, write them down, and maintain focus. If you are advancing in your career, maintain your curiosity, strive to comprehend, and enhance your personal brand. When you retire, celebrate all you have accomplished, mentor others, enjoy time with your grandchildren, garden, and do what you love. Remember, as you serve others, you will never feel insignificant. The world needs you.

Let Us Stay Connected

Thank you for taking this journey of transformation with me. I would love to continue walking alongside you as you grow in your purpose.

You can connect with me and stay updated through the following platforms:

Facebook: Nova Pearson Kopp

Instagram: @NovaPearsonKopp

LinkedIn: Nova Kopp, Ph.D.
Email: TransformationAtAnyAgeCoach@gmail.com
Phone: 678-646-4683

I also offer personal coaching, group workshops, virtual events, and speaking engagements for churches, schools, and community organizations. If you're interested in booking me for an event or joining a coaching group, feel free to reach out directly.

Let us keep growing—one step, one season, and one transformation at a time.

Prayer

Dear Heavenly Father:

Thank You for guiding me through this journey of transformation. I am grateful for the wisdom You provide and the strength You give me each day.

Please help me to pursue my growth with intention and perseverance. Strengthen my mind, body, spirit, and finances as I walk this path. Please help me remember that I am never alone. You are my anchor, my refuge, and my guide.

When doubt and fear try to sabotage my progress, help me remember that You have equipped me with everything I need. Let Your Word serve as my guiding light, shedding light on my path even during the challenging moments.

Please help me to release my past, no matter how painful, and focus on the future You have planned for me. May I plant seeds of kindness, love, and faith every day, and may my life reflect Your light to others.

With love and gratitude,

Nova Kopp

www.ingramcontent.com/pod-product-compliance
Lightning Source LLC
Chambersburg PA
CBHW071725120626
46550CB00002B/389